THOUSAND YEARS OF LOVE POETRY

— Edited by Fiona Pagett —

CHAUCER PRESS
LONDON

Published by Chaucer Press
an imprint of the Caxton Publishing Group
20 Bloomsbury Street
London WC1B 3JH

ISBN 1 904449 05 0

Designed and produced for Chaucer Press
by Savitri Books Ltd

KRISHNA, THE DIVINE LOVER (DETAIL)

CONTENTS

LANDSCAPE NEAR BERN, FIODOR MATVEEV (DETAIL)

INTRODUCTION

Despite its title, the poems in this collection span nearly three thousand years, although after the end of the classical period we have a lull about a millennium before the troubadour emerges in southern France. As might be expected from a timespan of this magnitude, every possible aspect of love features here – fulfilled, unrequited or simply silent; rapturous, angry or despairing; passionate and erotic or calm and contented. This range of feelings spans the continents and the centuries. The book begins with the ancient Greek Sappho lamenting that the invincible love-god Eros has her in his power again, and ends with the Englishman James Fenton grieving because 'Nothing I do will make you love me more'. In between, Keats writes of 'La Belle Dame Sans Merci' who has him in thrall, and Oscar Wilde regrets the fact that he has abandoned wisdom and self-control in order 'to drift with every passion till my soul is a stringèd lute on which all winds can play'. The lover's powerlessness in the grip of love is a theme that the reader will find again and again.

The suffering of the poet also looms large. For the medieval writers following the conventions of 'courtly love', the object of their passion was traditionally virtuous, unobtainable, cold and cruel. Writing in the sixteenth century, the French poet Pierre de Ronsard warns Hélène (who rejects him steadfastly through 142 sonnets) that she will regret her decision when she is an old maid: 'But you, a crone, will crouch beside the hearth, mourning my love and all your proud disdain.' A generation or so later, Edmund Spenser wonders, 'My love is like to ice, and I to fire: How comes it then that this her cold so great is not dissolved through my so hot desire?' And in the next century Robert Herrick, is no more fortunate, not daring even to ask Electra for a kiss: 'No, no, the utmost share of my desire shall be only to kiss that air that lately kissèd thee.'

But it is not all bad news. Philip Sidney writes of the excellent bargain whereby 'My true love has my heart, and I have his' and Sir John Suckling takes a more robust attitude: 'If of herself she will not love, nothing can make her. The devil take her!'

Women poets are all too often the victims of male infidelity. 'Dearer than all the world he is to me; But he regards not love nor courtesy,' writes Beatrice de Die in the twelfth century. A Japanese empress writing in the fourteenth century of a love affair that has ended muses 'He made no promise – so I try to tell myself not to be bitter'; while six hundred years later and thousands of miles away, Anne Sexton is definitely bitter about a lover returning to his wife: 'As for me,' she says, 'I am a watercolour. I wash off.' On the other hand, Anne Bradstreet is able to write to her 'dear and loving husband', 'If ever two were one, then surely we' and Elizabeth Barrett Browning to begin her famous poem, 'How do I love thee? Let me count the ways.'

Lovers are, of course, also separated by death, and there are few poems in this collection more poignant than Amy Lowell's 'Patterns', in which a woman, admiring the patterns of her dress and her garden as she happily awaits her fiancé's returns from the war, learns instead that he has been killed. The poem ends with the heartfelt cry, 'Christ! What are patterns for?'

People in the throes of love, whether happy or unhappy, do not always appear in the most flattering light. There is selfishness here, there is self-pity and there is spite. But anyone who has ever loved and lost will have some fellow feeling for the sufferers. And going hand in hand with these baser emotions we find an uplifting strength in adversity, dignity, irony and occasionally – just occasionally– real joy.

LOVE POETRY

SAPPHO (7TH CENTURY BC)

Sappho lived on the Greek island of Lesbos, whose women had the reputation of being the most beautiful in the world (see under Catullus, page 14). Only fragments of her poetry survive, but their uninhibited passion speaks to us down the centuries.

She was like that sweetest apple
That ripened highest on the tree,
That the harvesters couldn't reach,
And pretended they forgot…
Like the mountain hyacinth trod underfoot
By shepherd men, its flower purple on the ground.

Percussion, salt and honey,
A quivering in the thighs;
He shakes me all over again,
Eros who cannot be thrown,
Who stalks on all fours
Like a beast.

Eros makes me shiver again
Strengthless in the knees,
Eros gall and honey,
Snake-sly, invincible.

❦❧❦

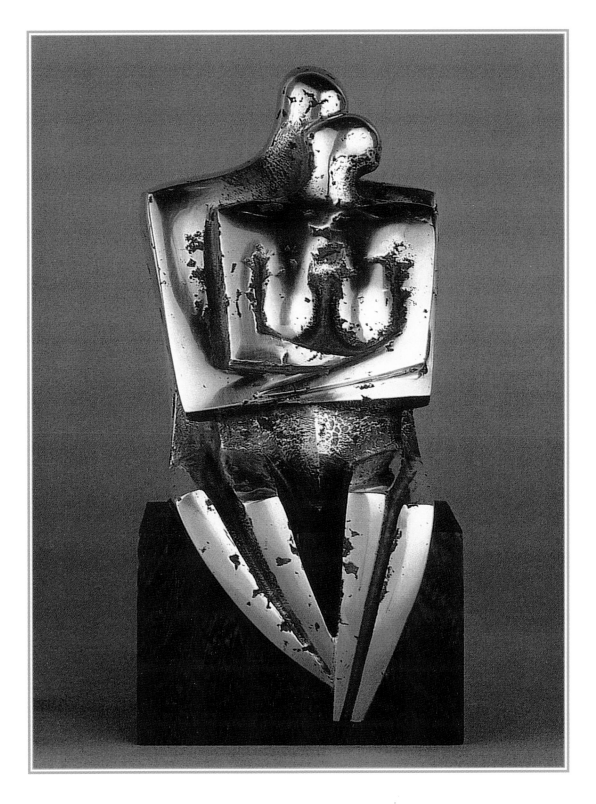

THE COUPLE, WUMA MBAMBILA NDOMBASI

LOVE POETRY

CAIUS VALERIUS CATULLUS (87– c.45BC)

The great romantic and erotic poet of ancient Rome, Catullus spent much of his life in thrall to the lady he nicknamed Lesbia (a compliment derived from the fact that the women of Lesbos were supposed to be the most beautiful in the world). Over a period of years, the capricious Lesbia played fast and loose with Catullus's passion, as can be seen from the rapture and despair of these verses.

TO LESBIA

Love, my Lesbia, while we live;
Value all the cross advice
That the surly greybeards give
At a single farthing's price.

Suns that set again may rise;
We, when once our fleeting light,
Once our day in darkness dies,
Sleep in one eternal night.

Give me kisses thousand-fold,
Add to them a hundred more;
Other thousands still be told
Other hundreds o'er and o'er.

But, with thousands when we burn,
Mix, confuse the sums at last,
That we may not blushing learn
All that have between us past.

None shall know to what amount
Envy's due for so much bliss;
None – for none shall ever count
All the kisses we will kiss.

To Lesbia on her Falsehood

To me alone, thou said'st, thy love was true,
And true should be, though Jove himself might woo.
I loved thee, Lesbia, not as rakes may prize
The favourite wanton who has pleased their eyes;
Mine was a tender glow, a purer zeal;
'Twas all the parent for the child can feel.

Thy common falsehood now, thyself I know;
And though my frame with fiercer heat may glow,
Yet Lesbia's vile and worthless in my sight,
Compared with Lesbia once my heart's delight;
Nor wonder passion's unrestrain'd excess
Makes me desire thee more, but love thee less.

Lesbia's Vow of Constancy
(addressed to herself)

Dost thou, my life, a tender bond propose
Of lasting truth and constant love's delights?
Gods grant, that truly from thy heart it flows,
And nerve that heart to keep the faith it plights!

A hunter's skilled where to spread his nets for the stag, senses
In which glen the wild boar lurks.
A fowler's familiar with copses, an expert angler
Knows the richest shoaling-grounds for fish.
You too, so keen to establish some long-term relationship,
Must learn, first, where girl is to be found.
Your search need not take you – believe me – on an overseas voyage:
A short enough trek will bring you to your goal.
True, Perseus fetched home Andromeda from the coloured Indies,
While Phrygian Paris abducted Helen in Greece,
But Rome can boast of so many and such dazzling beauties
You'd swear the whole world's talent was gathered here…
Venus indeed still haunts
Her son Aeneas' foundation. If you like budding adolesce
Any number of (guaranteed) maidens are here to delight
Your roving eye. You prefer young women? They'll charm
By the thousand, you won't know which to choose.
And if you happen to fancy a more mature, experienced
Age-group, believe me, they show up in droves.

According to the principles of medieval chivalry, one of the first duties of a knight was to protect women. From this developed the concept of courtly love, in which serving the lady he loves becomes the object of a knight's earthly life, going hand in hand with his commitment to serving God. Out of the tradition of courtly love, which reached the height of its popularity in medieval Provence, grew a band of composers and performers known as troubadours, whose songs reflect the reverence a knight felt for his lady and his despair at her cruelty.
Countess Beatrice de Die is the only lady-troubadour whose poems survive in any

quantity and they, too, tell the story of a love affair that begins in rapture and ends, with this extract, in misery because of the beloved's cruelty.

BERNART OF VENTARDORN (c.1125-c.1200)

With joy I now begin my song,
With joy I end and finish too,
And if the end be good and true
Then the beginning can't be wrong.
Since that for the good beginning
Joy and happiness I'm winning,
Therefore to thank the good end would be meet,
For all good things I hear praised when complete.

Joy masters and o'erpowers me,
And verily I marvel how
I can refrain from telling now
What joy is mine, and gaiety
But 'tis seldom that a lover
Dares his passion to discover;
Fear of offending her makes me so meek,
My courage fails me and I dare not speak

I am well skilled in this one thing:
That willingly I always lie
To any man who asks me why
I'm happy, and rejoice and sing,
He acts foolishly and blindly
Who, when Love looks on him kindly,

Unto another dares his love to tell
– Unless he knows that he can serve him well.

I hate a meddling man above
All others, and it seems to me
There is no worse discourtesy
Than prying into others' love.
Envious, what are you enjoying,
Me thus troubling and annoying?
Let all men strive their duty to fulfil;
You gain no joy by treating me so ill.

Courage will oft a lady save
From spiteful and malicious men,
For if her heart do fail her then
She scarcely can be good or brave.
Her whom I shall love for ever
I implore that she will never
Be changed or moved by slanderous words, for I
Of jealousy can make the jealous die.

I never thought of treachery
When from her lips I tasted bliss,
But death she dealt me with a kiss,
And if one more she gives not me,
As by Peleus' weapon smitten
Shall I be, for it is written
That no man could be healed whom it had hit
Unless his wound was struck again by it.

Fair lady, I am conquered quite

By your great beauty and your fair

Red laughing lips and gracious air,

Sweet smile and eyes than stars more bright,

For, 'mong all I see around me

None so fair as you I've found me.

The gentlest lady in the world I woo,

My eyes are dazzled when I look on you.

Love with joy indeed has crowned me

Who to such a lady's bound me

That those who praise her cannot speak more true,

And those who blame, a worse deed cannot do.

ARNAUT DANIEL (fl. 1180-1200)

To this tune that sounds so gaily

Words I fashion of the rarest;

True and certain will they be

When my file has shaped them neatly;

Love makes smooth and gilds full fairly

This my song, inspired by one

Who is noble altogether.

Better, purer grow I daily,

Seeing her who is the fairest,

This I tell you openly.

Head to foot I'm hers completely

And though cold winds blow not rarely,
My heart's love, like summer sun,
Keeps me warm in wintry weather.

Thousand masses I've attended,
Lights of wax and oil I'm burning,
That God may to pity move
Her 'gainst whom I can't protect me;
When I see her golden tresses
And her figure fair and slim,
Nought on earth so much I treasure.

My heart's love on her's expended
And I ever fear her spurning,
So that love my loss may prove.
In a flood of love she's wrecked me
Which, ne'er ebbing, still me blesses,
I obey her every whim,
Write her songs in bounteous measure.

Emperor I would not make me,
Nor the Papacy desire,
If from her I had to part
For whose sake my heart is breaking.
If to kiss me soon she pleases
Not, 'twill kill me, I declare,
And her soul to hell deliver.

BEATRICE DE DIE (MID 12TH CENTURY)

It is in vain, this silence I must break;
The fault of him I love moves me to speak.
Dearer than all the world he is to me;
But he regards not love nor courtesy,
Nor wisdom, nor my worth, nor all my beauty –
He has deceived me. Such my fate should be,
If I had failed to him in loving duty.

Oh, strange and past belief that in disdain
Your heart, oh friend, should look upon my pain;
That now another love should conquer you,
For all that I may say, that I may do!
Have you forgotten the sweet first communion
Of our two hearts? Now sorely would I rue
If by my guilt were caused this last disunion.

The noble worth, the valour you possess,
Your fame and beauty add to my distress.
For far and near the noble ladies all,
If love can move them, listen to your call.
But you, my friend, whose soul is keenest-sighted,
Must know who loves you, and is true withal.
And ah! remember now the troth we plighted.

᪣

SMALL BOUQUET, JAN BRUEGHEL (DETAIL)

LOVE POETRY

EMPEROR FUSHIMI (1265-1317)

In addition to being a talented poet and calligrapher, Emperor Fushimi was an enthusiastic patron of the arts and his court was the home of many young and innovative poets. Deposed from power at the age of thirty-three, he compiled an anthology, Gyokuyoshu, which contained 2796 examples of the new style of poetry that flourished during his reign.

WAITING FOR LOVE

Come to me tonight –
and if all your promises
on nights to come
should turn out to be lies,
then let them be lies.

LOVE, WITH BOAT AS AN IMAGE

In a hidden bay
an abandoned boat lies rotting
against the shoreline –
just as my heart lies broken
out of yearning for you.

A LOVE POEM

You – bird flying off

into the evening sky:
not so long ago
I too was hurrying away
to the same place every night.

EMPRESS EIFUKU (1271-1342)

Fushimi's wife for thirty years, Eifuku shared with her husband a passion for poetry.
After his death, she carried on his work as a patron of the arts.

A LOVE POEM

He made no promise –
so I try to tell myself
not to be bitter
until this long night too
ends with a lonely dawn.

UNREQUITED LOVE

If even now
in the midst of rejection
I still love him so,
then what would be my feelings
if he were to love me back?

LOVE POEMS (extract)

I got used to him –
and was gradually drawn along
by a growing fondness,
until now the time has come
that I can hate him no more.

MIRABAI (1498-1565)

Mirabai is one of the best known representatives of the Hindu religious movement known as 'bhakti' which grew around the cult of the God Krishna. The protagonists of bhakti *sought to establish a closer personal relationship with God. Mirabai was born in an aristocratic Rajput family and married into another powerful royal household. It is said that during her childhood she experienced a vision of Lord Krishna. This event had such an impact on her that from then on she considered herself a bride of the Lord and dedicated her life to him. She eventually left her royal husband to lead the life of a religous mendicant, composing and singing poems of an extraordinary intensity, proclaiming her passion and dedication to* Giridhara Gopal – *another name for Lord Krishna. The poems are a heady mixture of womanly passionate longing and mystical love. They are as popular today as they ever were and are sung by village women as well as by distinguished Indian classical singers.*

I AM PALE WITH LONGING FOR MY BELOVED

I am pale with longing for my beloved;
People believe I am ill.
Seizing on every possible pretext,
I try to meet him 'by accident.'

KRISHNA DALLYING WITH THE *GOPIS* (HERD-GIRLS)

They have sent for a country doctor;

He grabs my arm and prods it;

How can he diagnose my pain?

It's in my heart that I am afflicted.

Go home, country doctor,

Don't address me by my name;

It's the name of God that has wounded me,

Don't force your medicines on me.

The sweetness of his lips is a pot of nectar,

That's the only curd for which I crave;

Mira's Lord is *Giridhara Gopal*.

He will feed me nectar again and again.

SIR THOMAS WYATT (1503-1542)

Thomas Wyatt had a chequered career at the court of Henry VIII, where he was favoured by Catharine of Aragon but later imprisoned, perhaps on suspicion of having been a lover of Anne Boleyn. His work is now overlooked by many, but he is regarded by some as the precursor of many greater English love poets.

FORGET NOT YET
The Lover Beseecheth his Mistress not to Forget his Steadfast Faith and True Intent

Forget not yet the tried entent

Of such a truth as I have meant;

My great travail so gladly spent,
Forget not yet!

Forget not yet when first began
The weary life ye know, since when
The suit, the service, none tell can;
Forget not yet!

Forget not yet the great assays,
The cruel wrong, the scornful ways,
The painful patience in denays,
Forget not yet!

Forget not, yet forget not this –
How long ago hath been, and is,
The mind that never meant amiss –
Forget not yet!

Forget not then thine own approved,
The which so long hath thee so loved,
Whose steadfast faith yet never moved:
Forget not this!

THE APPEAL
An Earnest Suit to his Unkind Mistress, not to Forsake Him

And wilt thou leave me thus?
Say nay, say nay, for shame! –
To save thee from the blame

Of all my grief and grame
And wilt thou leave me thus?
Say nay! say nay!

And wilt thou leave me thus,
That hath loved thee so long
In wealth and woe among:
And is thy heart so strong
As for to leave me thus?
Say nay! say nay!

And wilt thou leave me thus,
That hath given thee my heart
Never for to depart
Neither for pain nor smart:
And wilt thou leave me thus?
Say nay! say nay!

And wilt thou leave me thus,
And have no more pity
Of him that loveth thee?
Alas, thy cruelty!
And wilt thou leave me thus?
Say nay! say nay!

A REVOCATION

What should I say?
– Since Faith is dead,

And Truth away
From you is fled?
Should I be led
With doubleness?
Nay! nay! mistress.

I promised you,
And you prornised me,
To be as true
As I would be.
But since I see
Your double heart,
Farewell my part!

Thought for to take
'Tis not my mind;
But to forsake
One so unkind;
And as I find
So will I trust.
Farewell, unjust!

Can ye say nay
But that you said
That I alway
Should be obeyed?
And – thus betrayed
Or that I wist!
Farewell, unkist!

LOVE POETRY

PIERRE DE RONSARD (1524-1585)

Ronsard, the greatest French poet of the sixteenth century, started his career as a soldier, but was forced to abandon this occupation because of deafness. He subsequently became the most prominent of the Pléiade, a group of writers whose aim was to raise the status of French as a literary language. A favourite at the court of Charles IX and Henri III, he is best known for his love poems to three women: Cassandre, a chaste lady who inspired poems that speak of the purity of love; Marie, a peasant girl, for whom his feelings were more earthy; and, later in life, Hélène, a noblewoman in the service of Henri III's queen, Catherine de Medici. The following are two of the 142 sonnets addressed to Hélène, all of which extolled her beauty and complained of her cruelty and the poet's hopeless passion.

Shall I your beauties with the moon compare?
She's faithless, you a single purpose own.
Or to the general sun, who everywhere
goes common with his light; you walk alone?
And you are such that envy must despair
of finding in my praise aught to condone,
who have no likeness since there's naught as fair,
yourself your god, your star, Fate's overtone.
Those mad or rash, who make some other woman
your rival, hurt themselves when they would hurt you,
so far your excellence their dearth outpaces.
Either your body shields some noble demon,
or mortal you image immortal virtue,
or Pallas you or first among the Graces.

OPPOSITE. LANDSCAPE NEAR BERN, FIODOR MATVEEV (DETAIL)

When you are old, at evening candle-lit
beside the fire bending to your wool,
read out my verse and murmur, 'Ronsard writ
this praise for me when I was beautiful.'
And not a maid but, at the sound of it,
though nodding at the stitch on broidered stool,
will start awake, and bless love's benefit
whose long fidelities bring Time to school.
I shall be thin and ghost beneath the earth
by myrtle shade in quiet after pain,
but you, a crone, will crouch beside the hearth
mourning my love and all your proud disdain.
And since what comes to-morrow who can say?
Live, pluck the roses of the world to-day.

❧❧

EDMUND SPENSER (c.1552-1599)

The Elizabethan and Jacobean eras combined to produce the golden age of English poetry.
Spenser, best known as the author of the epic Faerie Queene, *is often difficult for*
modern readers to appreciate because of his frequent references to the classical subjects
that would have been familiar to any educated person of his day. This poem is much more
straightforward, and marks an interesting transition from the respectful tradition of
courtly love to the more passionate love poems of the next generation.
Here the lady is still cold and cruel, but the poet admits to more
violent passion than would have been acceptable
to the troubadours.

MY LOVE IS LIKE TO ICE

My love is like to ice, and I to fire:
How comes it then that this her cold so great
Is not dissolved through my so hot desire,
But harder grows the more I her entreat?
Or how comes it that my exceeding heat
Is not allayed by her heart-frozen cold,
But that I burn much more in boiling sweat,
And feel my flames augmented manifold?
What more miraculous thing may be told,
That fire, which all things melts, should harden ice,
And ice, which is congealed with senseless cold,
Should kindle fire by wonderful device?
Such is the power of love in gentle mind,
That it can alter all the course of kind.

❧❧❧

SIR PHILIP SIDNEY (1554-1586)

A friend and contemporary of Walter Raleigh, Philip Sidney was a soldier and diplomat as well as a writer. He also became a patron of the arts at a young age: Spenser's 'Shepheardes Calendar', published when Sidney was only twenty-five, is one of a number of works dedicated to him. Many romantic stories have grown up about his heroic death from a wound received in battle in the Netherlands, giving him a posthumous reputation as the perfect Renaissance gentleman.

THE BARGAIN

My true love hath my heart, and I have his,
By just exchange one for another given:
I hold his dear, and mine he cannot miss,
There never was a better bargain driven:
My true love hath my heart, and I have his.
His heart in me keeps him and me in one,
My heart in him his thoughts and senses guides:
He loves my heart, for once it was his own,
I cherish his because in me it bides:
My true love hath my heart, and I have his.

CHRISTOPHER MARLOWE (1564-1593)

*Twenty-nine-year-old Christopher Marlowe had already shown great brilliance
as a playwright and poet when he was killed in a south London tavern.
His plays, which contain the best pre-Shakespearian examples of blank verse,
include* Dr Faustus, Edward II *and* The Jew of Malta, *and in addition to his
own poetry he translated a number of classical authors, including Ovid and Lucan.
The circumstances of his death remain mysterious, some maintaining that he was
merely involved in a drunken brawl, others that he was murdered, perhaps because
of his allegedly blasphemous beliefs.*

THE PASSIONATE SHEPHERD TO HIS LOVE

Come live with me and be my Love,
And we will all the pleasures prove

That hills and valleys, dales and fields,
Or woods or steepy mountain yields.

And we will sit upon the rocks,
And see the shepherds feed their flocks
By shallow rivers, to whose falls
Melodious birds sing madrigals.

And I will make thee beds of roses
And a thousand fragrant posies;
A cap of flowers, and a kirtle
Embroider'd all with leaves of myrtle.

A gown made of the finest wool
Which from our pretty lambs we pull;
Fair-linèd slippers for the cold,
With buckles of the purest gold.

A belt of straw and ivy-buds
With coral claps and amber studs:
And if these pleasures may thee move,
Come live with me and be my Love.

The shepherd swains shall dance and sing
For thy delight each May morning:
If these delights thy mind may move,
Then live with me and be my Love.

ଌ▲ଌ▲

HER REPLY
(WRITTEN BY SIR WALTER RALEIGH)

If all the world and love were young,
And truth in every shepherd's tongue,
These pretty pleasures might me move
To live with thee and be thy Love.

But Time drives flocks from field to fold;
When rivers rage and rocks grow cold;
And Philomel becometh dumb;
The rest complains of cares to come.

The flowers do fade, and wanton fields
To wayward Winter reckoning yields:
A honey tongue, a heart of gall,
Is fancy's spring, but sorrow's fall.

Thy gowns, thy shoes, thy beds of roses,
Thy cap, thy kirtle, and thy posies,
Soon break, soon wither – soon forgotten,
In folly ripe, in reason rotten.

Thy belt of straw and ivy-buds,
Thy coral clasps and amber studs, –
All these in me no means can move
To come to thee and be thy Love.

But could youth last, and love still breed,

OPPOSITE. THE BOUQUET OF IRISES, JAN BRUEGHEL

Had joys no date, nor age no need,
Then these delights my mind might move
To live with thee and be thy Love.

WILLIAM SHAKESPEARE (1564-1616)

Shakespeare is by common consent the greatest playwright and poet of the English language. He introduced many short songs into his comedies, some sung by the 'clown' character such as Feste in Twelfth Night, *others designed as commentaries on the action or merely as an interlude, as in the song from* The Merchant of Venice *included here. This is sung while Bassanio is pondering which of the caskets in front of him he should choose in order to win the right to marry Portia. Shakespeare's 150 sonnets include some of the most beautiful love poems ever written.*

SILVIA (from *Two Gentlemen of Verona*)

Who is Silvia? What is she?
That all our swains commend her?
Holy, fair, and wise is she;
The heaven such grace did lend her,
That she might admirèd be.

Is she kind as she is fair?
For beauty lives with kindness:
Love doth to her eyes repair,
To help him of his blindness;
And, being help'd, inhabits there.

Then to Silvia let us sing,

That Silvia is excelling;

She excels each mortal thing

Upon the dull earth dwelling:

To her let us garlands bring.

LOVE (from *The Merchant of Venice*)

Tell me where is Fancy bred,

Or in the heart or in the head?

How begot, how nourishèd?

Reply, reply. It is engender'd in the eyes,

With gazing fed; and Fancy dies

Let us all ring Fancy's knell:

I'll begin it, – Ding, dong, bell!

Ding, dong, bell!

SWEET-AND-TWENTY (from *Twelfth Night*)

O Mistress mine, where are you roaming?

O, stay and hear! your true love's coming,

That can sing both high and low:

Trip no further, pretty sweeting;

Journeys end in lovers meeting,

Every wise man's son doth know.

What is love? 'tis not hereafter;

Present mirth hath present laughter;

What's to come is still unsure:

In delay there lies no plenty;
Then come kiss me, sweet-and-twenty!
Youth's a stuff will not endure.

SONNET 18

Shall I compare thee to a Summer's day?
Thou art more lovely and more temperate:
Rough winds do shake the darling buds of May,
And Summer's lease hath all too short a date:
Sometime too hot the eye of heaven shines,
And often is his gold complexion dimm'd;
And every fair from fair sometime declines,
By chance or nature's changing course untrimm'd:
But thy eternal Summer shall not fade
Nor lose possession of that fair thou owest;
Nor shall Death brag thou wanderest in his shade,
When in eternal lines to time thou growest:
So long as men can breathe, or eyes can see,
So long lives this, and this gives life to thee.

SONNET 30

When to the Sessions of sweet silent thought
I summon up remembrance of things past,
I sigh the lack of many a thing I sought,
And with old woes new wail my dear time's waste:
Then can I drown an eye, unused to flow,

For precious friends hid in death's dateless night,
And weep afresh love's long-since-cancell'd woe,
And moan th'expense of many a vanish'd sight:
Then can I grieve at grievances foregone,
And heavily from woe to woe tell o'er
The sad account of fore-bemoanèd moan,
Which I new pay as if not paid before.
But if the while I think on thee, dear friend,
All losses are restored and sorrows end.

SONNET 116

Let me not to the marriage of true minds
Admit impediments. Love is not love
Which alters when it alteration finds,
Or bends with the remover to remove:
Oh no, it is an ever fixèd mark
That looks on tempests and is never shaken;
It is the star to every wandering bark,
Whose worth's unknown, although his height be taken.
Love's not Time's fool, though rosy lips and cheeks
Within his bending sickle's compass come;
Love alters not with his brief hours and weeks,
But bears it out even to the edge of doom.
If this be error and upon me proved,
I never writ, nor no man ever loved.

LOVE POETRY

THOMAS CAMPION (1567?-1619)

Thomas Campion was a musician as well as a poet, setting a number of his own works to music. His verse cannot stand comparison with that of his greatest contemporaries, but this simple ditty retains its appeal.

CHERRY-RIPE

There is a garden in her face
Where roses and white lilies blow;
A heavenly paradise is that place,
Wherein all pleasant fruits do flow;
There cherries grow which none may buy
Till 'Cherry-ripe' themselves do cry.

Those cherries fairly do enclose
Of orient pearls a double row,
Which when her lovely laughter shows,
They look like rose-buds fill'd with snow;
Yet them nor peer nor prince can buy
Till 'Cherry-ripe' themselves do cry.

Her eyes like angels watch them still;
Her brows like bended bows to stand,
Threat'ning with piercing frowns to kill
All that attempt with eye or hand
Those sacred cherries to come nigh,
Till 'Cherry-ripe' themselves do cry.

OPPOSITE. THE BOUQUET OF LILIES, JAN BRUEGHEL (DETAIL)

LOVE POETRY

BEN JONSON (1573-1637)

Another of the great 'Renaissance men' of the era, Jonson was a soldier, dramatist, poet and scholar, more highly esteemed in his day than Shakespeare. After an unsettled early career which involved a period of imprisonment after killing a fellow actor in a duel, he became established at the court of James I and was granted a pension that made him, to all intents and purposes, Britain's first Poet Laureate. His reputation dwindled in the eighteenth century as Shakespeare became more highly esteemed, but he has now been restored to the position he deserves and his satirical comedy Volpone, *in particular, is frequently performed.*

TO CELIA

Drink to me only with thine eyes,
And I will pledge with mine;
Or leave a kiss but in the cup
And I'll not look for wine.
The thirst that from the soul doth rise
Doth ask a drink divine;
But might I of Jove's nectar sup,
I would not change for thine.

I sent thee late a rosy wreath,
Not so much honouring thee
As giving it a hope that there
It could not wither'd be;
But thou thereon didst only breathe,
And sent'st it back to me;
Since when it grows, and smells, I swear,
Not of itself but thee!

LOVE POETRY

ROBERT HERRICK (1591-1674)

Herrick's most famous poem, 'To the Virgins, to Make Much of Time' ('Gather ye rosebuds while ye may') is an exhortation to his lady love not to waste time in maidenly modesty. Here he returns to the more courtly tradition, in which his lady, as he himself phrases it 'may command him anything'.

TO ELECTRA

I dare not ask a kiss,
I dare not beg a smile,
Lest having that, or this,
I might grow proud the while.

No, no, the utmost share
Of my desire shall be
Only to kiss that air
That lately kissèd thee.

TO ANTHEA, WHO MAY COMMAND HIM ANYTHING

Bid me to live, and I will live
Thy Protestant to be;
Or bid me love, and I will give
A loving heart to thee.

A heart as soft, a heart as kind,
A heart as sound and free
As in the whole world thou canst find;
That heart I'll give to thee.

Bid that heart stay, and it will stay
To honour thy decree:
Or bid it languish quite away,
And 't shall do so for thee.

Bid me to weep, and I will weep
While I have eyes to see:
And, having none, yet will I keep
A heart to weep for thee.

Bid me despair, and I'll despair
Under that cypress-tree:
Or bid me die, and I will dare
E'en death to die for thee.

Thou art my life, my love, my heart,
The very eyes of me:
And hast command of every part
To live and die for thee.

Two anonymous poems from the early seventeenth-century.

THERE IS A LADY SWEET AND KIND

There is a Lady sweet and kind,
Was never face so pleased my mind;
I did but see her passing by,
And yet I love her till I die.

PORTRAIT OF FELICIANA BAYEU, FRANISCO BAYEU

Her gesture, motion, and her smiles,
Her wit, her voice my heart beguiles,
Beguiles my heart, I know not why,
And yet I love her till I die.

Cupid is wingèd and doth range,
Her country so my love doth change:
But change she earth, or change she sky,
Yet will I love her till I die.

LOVE NOT ME FOR COMELY GRACE

Love not me for comely grace,
For my pleasing eye or face,
Nor for any outward part,
No, nor for a constant heart:
For these may fail or turn to ill,
So thou and I shall sever:
Keep, therefore, a true woman's eye,
And love me still but know not why –
So hast thou the same reason still
To doat upon me ever!

SIR JOHN SUCKLING (1609-1642)

A member of the group loosely described as 'Cavalier poets', Suckling's career was cut short by the onset of Civil War in England. A supporter of the Royalist cause, he fled to France, where he may have committed suicide.

LOVE POETRY

THE CONSTANT LOVER

Out upon it, I have loved
Three whole days together!
And am like to love three more,
If it prove fair weather.

Time shall moult away his wings
Ere he shall discover
In the whole wide world again
Such a constant lover.

But the spite on't is, no praise
Is due at all to me:
Love with me had made no stays,
Had it any been but she.

Had it any been but she,
And that very face,
There had been at least ere this
A dozen dozen in her place.

WHY SO PALE AND WAN?

Why so pale and wan, fond lover?
Prithee, why so pale?
Will, when looking well can't move her,
Looking ill prevail?
Prithee, why so pale?

Why so dull and mute, young sinner?

Prithee, why so mute?

Will, when speaking well can't win her,

Saying nothing do't?

Prithee, why so mute?

Quit, quit for shame! This will not move;

This cannot take her.

If of herself she will not love,

Nothing can make her:

The devil take her!

ANNE BRADSTREET (1612-1672)

Considered the first American poet, Anne Bradstreet was born in England but within ten years of the Pilgrim Fathers' setting out she travelled to the fledging colony with her husband, who became Governor of Massachusetts. A committed Puritan, she wrote more about the next world than this one. This poem manages to convey both her deep religious faith and her devotion to her husband.

TO MY DEAR AND LOVING HUSBAND

If ever two were one, then surely we.

If ever man were lov'd by wife, then thee;

If ever wife was happy in a man,

Compare with me ye women if you can.

I prize thy love more than whole Mines of gold,

THE DANCE OF THE PEASANTS, PETER BRUEGEL

Or all the riches that the East doth hold.

My love is such that Rivers cannot quench,

Nor ought but love from thee give recompence.

Thy love is such I can no way repay,

The heavens reward thee manifold I pray.

Then while we live, in love lets so persever,

That when we live no more, we may live ever.

RICHARD LOVELACE (1618-1657)

Another of the 'Cavalier poets', Lovelace came of a wealthy family and as a young man was a member of Charles I's court. His support of the Royalist cause landed him in prison, where he wrote some of his finest poetry.

TO LUCASTA, GOING TO THE WARS

Tell me not, Sweet, I am unkind,

That from the nunnery

Of thy chaste breast and quiet mind

To war and arms I fly.

True, a new mistress now I chase,

The first foe in the field;

And with a stronger faith embrace

A sword, a horse, a shield.

Yet this inconstancy is such

As thou too shalt adore;

I could not love thee, Dear, so much,
Loved I not Honour more.

To Althea, from Prison

When Love with unconfinèd wings
Hovers within my gates;
And my divine Althea brings
To whisper at the grates;
When I lie tangled in her hair,
And fettered to her eye;
The Gods that wanton in the air
Know no such liberty.

When flowing cups run swiftly round
With no allaying Thames,
Our careless heads with roses bound
Our hearts with loyal flames;
When thirsty grief in wine we steep,
When healths and draughts go free,
Fishes that tipple in the deep
Know no such liberty.

When, like committed linnets, I
With shriller throat shall sing
The sweetness, mercy, majesty,
And glories of my King;
When I shall voice aloud how good
He is, how great should be,

Enlargèd winds that curl the flood
Know no such liberty.

Stone walls do not a prison make,
Nor iron bars a cage;
Minds innocent and quiet take
That for an hermitage;
If I have freedom in my love,
And in my soul am free;
Angels alone that soar above
Enjoy such liberty.

JOHN DRYDEN (1631-1700)

The Renaissance brought a great revival of interest in the Greek and Latin authors whose works had been largely neglected until Constantinople fell to the Turks in 1453. Christian monks then dispersed across Europe, carrying the contents of their libraries with them. The Neo-classical movement, of which Dryden was a prominent member, made it a rule to copy the style and conventions of these earlier writers.

FAREWELL, UNGRATEFUL TRAITOR

Farewell, ungrateful traitor,
Farewell, my perjured swain,
Let never injured creature
Believe a man again.
The pleasure of possessing

Surpasses all expressing,
But 'tis too short a blessing,
And love too long a pain.

'Tis easy to deceive us
In pity of your pain,
But when we love you leave us
To rail at you in vain.
Before we have descried it
There is no bliss beside it,

THE LOVE TOKEN, VALENTINA LERMONTOV

But she that once has tried it
Will never love again.

The passion you pretended
Was only to obtain,
But when the charm is ended
The charmer you disdain.
Your love by ours we measure
Till we have lost our treasure,
But dying is a pleasure,
When living is a pain.

SIR CHARLES SEDLEY (1639-1701)

A contemporary and friend of Dryden, Sedley combined a debauched private life with witty and polished literary works. Having been a courtier in the time of James II, he prudently transferred his allegiance to William III when James was deposed.

TO CELIA

Not, Celia, that I juster am
Or better than the rest!
For I would change each hour, like them,
Were not my heart at rest.

But I am tied to very thee
By every thought I have;

Thy face I only care to see,
Thy heart I only crave.

All that in woman is adored
In thy dear self I find –
For the whole sex can but afford
The handsome and the kind.

Why then should I seek further store,
And still make love anew?
When change itself can give no more,
'Tis easy to be true!

WILLIAM CONGREVE (1670-1729)

Congreve was born in Yorkshire and educated at Trinity College, Dublin, where he became a friend of Jonathan Swift. Returning to London, where he briefly practised law, he joined the same literary circles as Richard Steele, one of the founders of The Tatler *and* The Specator, *and Alexander Pope. He is best remembered for his plays* Love for Love *and* The Way of the World, *among the best surviving examples of Restoration comedies. He lost his sight towards the end of his life but lived in reasonable comfort thanks to a number of undemanding government posts. He is buried in Westminster Abbey.*

SONG

A nymph and a swain to Apollo once prayed,
The swain had been jilted, the nymph been betrayed,

Their intent was to try if this oracle knew
E'er a nymph that was chaste, or a swain that was true.

Apollo was mute, and had like t'have been posed,
But sagely at length he this secret disclosed:
He alone won't betray in whom none will confide,
And the nymph may be chaste that has never been tried.

JOHANN WOLFGANG VON GOETHE (1749-1832)

Johann Wolfgang von Goethe was born in Frankfurt-am-Main and is regarded as one of the greatest of German writers. Blessed with a multi-facetted talent: a poet, dramatist scientist and a court official, the directness and simplicity of his lyrical expression was to influence generations of German poets and writers. His poetry, whether in the dramas – Faust, *for one, or in his narrative poems:* Hermann and Dorothea – *finds its simplest and most delightful expression in his short lyrics. This is the genre which is illustrated here. The three poems are addressed to Lili Schönemann, with whom he became engaged in 1775. The poems point to a deep love between them, despite the difference in their character. They broke up their engagement a few month later, but it is obvious from Goethe's writings that, in spite of other loves and the many achievements of a long life, he never forgot Lili.*

NEW LOVE, NEW LIFE

Heart, my heart, oh why this feeling?
This oppression deep and sore?
Odd new life you are revealing,

Strange, I know your ways no more.

Gone is all that made you gladder,

Gone the grief that made you sadder,

Gone your zeal and peaceful bliss.

Ah, how could you come to this?

Does her form so charmed and youthful,

Like a newly opening flower,

Do her eyes so kindly truthful

Fetter you with endless power?

If at once no more I'd see her,

If I brace myself and flee her,

In a trice my feet will strain

To return to her again.

By this thread with magic laden

Which I cannot tear at all,

That beloved wanton maiden

Holds me, a reluctant thrall.

In her magic circle standing,

I must live at her commanding.

Ah, how great the change in me !

Love, oh love, oh set me free !

FROM THE HILLTOP

If I loved you not, beloved Lili,

What delight these eyes of yours would bring!

And yet if I loved you not, my Lili,

Where would I find joy in anything?

TO LILI
December, 1775

Lovely Lili, you were long
All my joy and all my song.
Now you're all my grief, and yetl,
Lili, you are still all my song.

RICHARD BRINSLEY SHERIDAN (1751-1816)

*Another poet better known as a playwright, Sheridan was also a theatrical manager,
prominent politician and brilliant orator. Irish-born, he became an ally of the great Whig
Charles James Fox and was elected Member of Parliament for Stafford in 1780. His
parliamentary reputation was established by some magnificent speeches against Warren
Hastings, whom the Whigs tried unsuccessfully to impeach on charges of
embezzlement during his service in India. Sheridan considered himself first and
foremost a parliamentarian, but he is remembered now as the author
of two great comedies of manners,* The Rivals *and*
A School for Scandal.

SONG

Here's to the maiden of bashful fifteen;
Here's to the widow of fifty;
Here's to the flaunting extravagant quean,
And here's to the housewife that's thrifty.

SELF-PORTRAIT WITH THE ARTIST'S WIFE, ANDREI MATVEEV

Chorus: Let the toast pass, –
Drink to the lass,
I'll warrant she'll prove an excuse for the glass.

Here's to the charmer whose dimples we prize;
Now to the maid who has none, sir:
Here's to the girl with a pair of blue eyes,
And here's to the nymph with but one, sir.

Here's to the maid with a bosom of snow;
Now to her that's as brown as a berry:
Here's to the wife with a face full of woe,
And now to the girl that is merry.

For let 'em be clumsy, or let 'em be slim,
Young or ancient, I care not a feather;
So fill a pint bumper quite up to the brim,
And let us e'en toast them together.

Chorus: Let the toast pass, –
Drink to the lass,
I'll warrant she'll prove an excuse for the glass.

WILLIAM BLAKE (1757-1827)

Blake was one of the early poetic rebels, rejecting conventional Christianity in favour of a belief that human beings, created in God's image, were by their nature divine. His best known works are Jerusalem, *which became a popular hymn, and* The Tyger.
Even his love poems have a mystical feel.

Never Seek to Tell thy Love

Never seek to tell thy love
Love that never told can be;
For the gentle wind does move
Silently, invisibly.

I told my love, I told my love,
I told her all my heart,
Trembling, cold, in ghastly fears –
Ah, she doth depart.

Soon as she was gone from me
A traveller came by
Silently, invisibly –
O, was no deny.

Robert Burns (1759-1796)

Many of Burns's poems are familiar the world over, particularly the New Year's Eve anthem Auld Lang Syne. *He employed many Scottish words and idioms which make some of his work unapproachable to non-Scots. This popular love poem is all the more appealing for its simplicity.*

My Love Is Like a Red Red Rose

My love is like a red red rose
That's newly sprung in June:

My love is like the melody
That's sweetly play'd in tune.

As fair art thou, my bonnie lass,
So deep in love am I:
And I will
love thee still, my dear,
Till a' the seas gang dry.

Till a' the seas gang dry, my dear,
And the rocks melt wi' the sun:
And I will love thee still, my dear,
While the sands o' life shall run.

And fare thee weel, my only love,
And fare thee weel a while!
And I will come again, my love,
Tho' it were ten thousand mile.

JAMES LEIGH HUNT (1784-1859)

In his lifetime Hunt was known mainly as the founder and editor of a number of journals in which he published the works of Charles Lamb, Keats, Byron and Shelley among many others. This poem does not, in fact, conform to the strict definition of a rondeau, which should have ten or thirteen lines and only two rhymes throughout. But it is another example of a poem being all the more touching for being very simple.

RONDEAU

Jenny kissed me when we met,

Jumping from the chair she sat in;

Time, you thief, who love to get

Sweets into your list, put that in!

Say I'm weary, say I'm sad,

Say that health and wealth have missed me,

Say I'm growing old, but add,

Jenny kissed me.

GEORGE GORDON, LORD BYRON (1788-1824)

Romanticism was rather more than a literary movement: born out of the political upheaval of the American and French Revolutions, it espoused many causes based on the ideals of liberty and equality. Romantic poets wrote about the relationship between man and nature, happy and unhappy love, childhood and the creative process itself. The movement, whose early exponents were Wordsworth and Coleridge, reached its peak with the brief but glorious careers of Byron, Keats and Shelley.

One morning in 1812, after the publication of the first part of 'Childe Harold's Pilgrimage', Byron, as he put it, 'awoke and found myself famous'. He spent a scandalous four years at the centre of London society before falling from grace and leaving England for good. He died of fever in Greece when he was only thirty-six.

SHE WALKS IN BEAUTY

She walks in beauty, like the night

Of cloudless climes and starry skies;

And all that's best of dark and bnght
Meet in her aspect and her eyes:
Thus mellowed to that tender light
Which heaven to gaudy day denies.

One shade the more, one ray the less,
Had half impaired the nameless grace
Which waves in every raven tress,
Or softly lightens o'er her face;
Where thoughts serenely sweet express
How pure, how dear their dwelling-place.

And on that cheek, and o'er that brow,
So soft, so calm, yet eloquent,
The smiles that win, the tints that glow,
But tell of days in goodness spent,
A mind at peace with all below,
A heart whose love is innocent!

PERCY BYSSHE SHELLEY (1792-1822)

Shelley packed a great deal of scandal into his short life, espousing atheism while he was still at Eton, quarrelling with his father when he was nineteen, eloping with a sixteen-year-old girl who bore him two children and, when that marriage broke down, eloping again, this time to Europe with Mary Godwin, who later found fame as the author of Frankenstein. After this, Shelley returned only briefly to England, spending his remaining years travelling in Europe and finally settling in Italy. He was drowned when the boat in which he was returning from a visit to Byron at Livorno was caught in a storm.

LOVE'S PHILOSOPHY

The fountains mingle with the river
And the rivers with the Ocean,
The winds of Heaven mix for ever
With a sweet emotion;
Nothing in the world is single;
All things by a law divine
In one spirit meet and mingle.
Why not I with thine? –

See the mountains kiss high Heaven
And the waves clasp one another,
No sister-flower would be forgiven
If it disdained its brother,
And the sunlight clasps the earth
And the moonbeams kiss the sea:
What is all this sweet work worth
If thou kiss not me?

JOHN KEATS (1795-1821)

Keats's life was even briefer than that of his friend Shelley and a great deal calmer. He was acquainted with Wordsworth and the critic William Hazlitt, both of whom influenced his work. The publication in 1817 of his first collection of poems provoked bitter criticism from Blackwood's *magazine, in which John Lockhart dismissed Keats and other poets of humble origins, including Leigh Hunt, as 'the Cockney school'. Over the course of the next three years, however,*

his reputation grew as his greatest poems appeared.
In 1818 Keats met and fell in love with Fanny Brawne, who inspired much
of his later work. They became engaged but never married. In 1820, Keats,
suffering from tuberculosis, travelled to Italy at Shelley's invitation.
Instead of staying with Shelley, he and his friend, the painter Joseph Severn,
settled in Rome, where Keats died in February of the following year.

La Belle Dame sans Merci

O what can ail thee, knight-at-arms,
Alone and palely loitering?
The sedge is wither'd from the lake,
And no birds sing.

O what can ail thee, knight-at-arms,
So haggard and so woe-begone?
The squirrel's granary is full,
And the harvest's done.

I see a lily on thy brow
With anguish moist and fever dew;
And on thy cheek a fading rose
Fast withereth too.

'I met a lady in the meads,
Full beautiful – a faery's child,
Her hair was long, her foot was light,
And her eyes were wild.

PORTRAIT OF VARVARA SUROVISEVA, FIODOR ROKOTOV.

'I made a garland for her head,
And bracelets too, and fragrant zone
She look'd at me as she did love,
And made sweet moan.

'I set her on my pacing steed
And nothing else saw all day long
For sideways would she lean, and sing
A faery's song.

'She found me roots of relish sweet,
And honey wild and manna dew,
And sure in language strange she said,
"I love thee true!"

'She took me to her elfin grot,
And there she wept and sigh'd full sore;
And there I shut her wild, wild eyes
With kisses four.

'And there she lullèd me asleep,
And there I dream'd – Ah! woe betide!
The latest dream I ever dream'd
On the cold hill's side.

'I saw pale kings and princes too,
Pale warriors, death-pale were they all;
Who cried – "La belle Dame sans Merci
Hath thee in thrall!"

'I saw their starved lips in the gloam
With horrid warning gapèd wide,
And I awoke and found me here
On the cold hill's side.

'And this is why I sojourn here
Alone and palely loitering,
Though the sedge is wither'd from the lake,
And no birds sing.'

TO FANNY BRAWNE

This living hand, now warm and capable
Of earnest grasping, would, if it were cold
And in the icy silence of the tomb,
So haunt thy days and chill thy dreaming nights
That thou wouldst wish thine own heart dry of blood
So in my veins red life might stream again,
And thou be conscience-calmed – see here it is –
I hold it towards you.

THOMAS HOOD (1799-1845)

A lesser poet of the Romantic school, Thomas Hood was prolific and popular in his day, moving in London literary circles with such luminaries as Lamb and Hazlitt. Much of his work was humorous and mildly satirical; 'The Song of the Shirt', an exposé of the evils of sweated labour, was very successful.

LOVE POETRY

TIME OF ROSES

It was not in the Winter
Our loving lot was cast;
It was the time of roses
We plucked them as we passed!

That churlish season never frowned
On early lovers yet:
O no – the world was newly crowned
With flowers when first we met!

'Twas twilight, and I bade you go,
But still you held me fast;
It was the time of roses
We plucked them as we passed!

VICTOR HUGO (1802-1885)

*One of the giants of French literature, Hugo was a prolific poet, novelist and playwright
and hailed in his youth as the leader of the Romantic Movement. Having also pursued a
career in politics, he prudently retired to the Channel Islands after a coup d'état in 1852.
Here he remained for almost twenty years, producing much of his best work,
including* Les Misérables. *After his return to Paris he became a popular senator and,
according to one nineteenth-century critic, his public funeral 'called forth a
demonstration of sorrow and enthusiasm such as had never
accompanied the remains of mortal man to their last resting-place'.
This poem is from one of his early works,* Les Feuilles d'automne.

TO A WOMAN

Child! if I were a king, my throne I would surrender,
My sceptre, and my car, and kneeling vavassours,
My golden crown, and porphyry baths, and consorts tender,
And fleets that fill the seas, and regal pomp and splendour,
All for one look of yours!

If I were God, the earth and luminous deeps that span it,
Angels and demons bowed beneath my word divine,
Chaos profound, with flanks of flaming gold and granite,
Eternity, and space, and sky and sun and planet,
All for one kiss of thine!

JAMES CLARENCE MANGAN (1803-1849)

Mangan's career was a tragic one, embittered by poverty and cut short by alcohol. But the best of his verse is powerful and moving.

THE LOVER'S FAREWELL

Slowly through the tomb-still streets I go –
Morn is dark, save one swart streak of gold –
Sullen rolls the far-off river's flow,
And the moon is very thin and cold.

Long and long before the house I stand
Where sleeps she, the dear, dear one I love –

All undreaming that I leave my land,
Mute and mourning, like the moon above!

Wishfully I stretch abroad mine arms
Towards the well-remembered casement-cell –
Fare thee well! Farewell thy virgin charms!
And thou stilly, stilly house, farewell!

And farewell the dear dusk little room,
Redolent of roses as a dell,
And the lattice that relieved its gloom –
And its pictured lilac walls, farewell!

Forth upon my path! I must not wait –
Bitter blows the fretful morning wind:
Warden, wilt thou softly close the gate
When thou knowest I leave my heart behind?

ELIZABETH BARRETT BROWNING (1806-1861)

Elizabeth Barrett eloped to Italy with her lover, the poet Robert Browning, fleeing from her disapproving father. They lived there, mostly in Florence, for the rest of her life, entertaining many literary and artistic visitors.

SONNETS FROM THE PORTUGUESE (extract)

If thou must love me, let it be for naught
Except for love's sake only. Do not say,

LOVE POETRY

'I love her for her smile – her look – her way

Of speaking gently, – for a trick of thought

That falls in well with mine, and certes brought

THE PROMISE, HENRY SCOTT TUKE

A sense of pleasant ease on such a day' –
For these things in themselves, Beloved, may
Be changed, or change for thee – and love, so wrought,
May be unwrought so. Neither love me for
Thine own dear pity's wiping my cheeks dry:
A creature might forget to weep, who bore
Thy comfort long, and lose thy love thereby!
But love me for love's sake, that evermore
Thou mayst love on, through love's eternity.

How Do I Love Thee? Let Me Count the Ways

How do I love thee? Let me count the ways.
I love thee to the depth and breadth and height
My soul can reach, when feeling out of sight
For the ends of being and ideal grace.
I love thee to the level of every day's
Most quiet need, by sun and candlelight.
I love thee freely, as men strive for right;
I love thee purely, as they tum from praise.
I love thee with the passion put to use
In my old griefs, and with my childhood's faith.
I love thee with a love I seemed to lose
With my lost saints – I love thee with the breath,
Smiles, tears, of all my life! – and, if God choose,
I shall but love thee better after death.

⁓

LOVE POETRY

ALFRED, LORD TENNYSON (1809-1892)

Tennyson's reputation and influence is unrivalled by any other nineteenth-century poet. He lived much of the latter part of his life on the Isle of Wight, where he received visits of homage from many writers and artists. He was also greatly admired by Queen Victoria, who appointed him Poet Laureate in 1850. His greatest work is undoubtedly 'In Memoriam', inspired by the early death of his friend Arthur Hallam, but he was one of the most prolific of all English poets and his verse includes Arthurian romance, classical subjects and many shorter poems inspired by English life and landscape.

COME INTO THE GARDEN, MAUD

Come into the garden, Maud,
For the black bat, night, has flown,
Come into the garden, Maud,
I am here at the gate alone;
And the woodbine spices are wafted abroad,
And the musk of the rose is blown.

For a breeze of morning moves,
And the planet of Love is on high,
Beginning to faint in the light that she loves
On a bed of daffodil sky,
To faint in the light of the sun she loves,
To faint in his light, and to die.

All night have the roses heard
The flute, violin, bassoon;
All night has the casement jessamine stirred

To the dancers dancing in tune;
Till a silence fell with the waking bird,
And a hush with the setting moon.

I said to the lily, 'There is but one
With whom she has heart to be gay.
When will the dancers leave her alone?
She is weary of dance and play.'
Now half to the setting moon are gone,
And half to the rising day;
Low on the sand and loud on the stone
The last wheel echoes away.

I said to the rose, 'The brief night goes
In babble and revel and wine.
O young lord-lover, what sighs are those,
For one that will never be thine?
But mine, but mine,' so I sware to the rose,
'For ever and ever, mine.'

And the soul of the rose went into my blood,
As the music clashed in the hall;
And long by the garden lake I stood,
For I heard your rivulet fall
From the lake to the meadow and on to the wood,
Our wood, that is dearer than all;

From the meadow your walks have left so sweet
That whenever a March-wind sighs

He sets the jewel-print of your feet
In violets blue as your eyes,
To the woody hollows in which we meet
And the valleys of Paradise.

The slender acacia would not shake
One long milk-bloom on the tree;
The white lake-blossom fell into the lake
As the pimpernel dozed on the lea;
But the rose was awake all night for your sake,
Knowing your promise to me;
The lilies and roses were all awake,
They sighed for the dawn and thee.

Queen rose of the rosebud garden of girls,
Come hither, the dances are done,
In gloss of satin and glimmer of pearls,
Queen lily and rose in one;
Shine out, little head, sunning over with curls,
To the flowers, and be their sun.

There has fallen a splendid tear
From the passion-flower at the gate.
She is coming, my dove, my dear;
She is coming, my life, my fate;
The red rose cries, 'She is near, she is near;'
And the white rose weeps, 'She is late;'
The larkspur listens, 'I hear, I hear;'
And the lily whispers, 'I wait.'

She is coming, my own, my sweet,
Were it ever so airy a tread,
My heart would hear her and beat,
Were it earth in an earthy bed;
My dust would hear her and beat,
Had I lain for a century dead;
Would start and tremble under her feet,
And blossom in purple and red.

IN MEMORIAM (extracts)

Dear friend, far off, my lost desire,
So far, so near in woe and weal;
O loved the most, when I most feel
There is a lower and a higher;

Known and unknown; human, divine;
Sweet human hand and lips and eye;
Dear heavenly friend that canst not die,
Mine, mine, forever, ever mine;

Strange friend, past, present, and to be;
Loved deeplier, darklier understood;
Behold, I dream a dream of good,
And mingle all the world with thee…

Love is and was my Lord and King
And in his presence I attend

OPPOSITE. SPRING, VICTOR BORTSOV-MUSATOV

To hear the tidings of my friend,
Which every hour his courtiers bring.

Love is and was my King and Lord
And will be, though as yet I keep
Within his court on earth, and sleep
Encompassed by his faithful guard,

And hear at times a sentinel
Who moves from place to place,
And whispers to the woods of space,
In the deep night, that all is well.

EDGAR ALLEN POE (1809-1849)

It may seem strange to find the author of Tales of the Grotesque and Arabesque *in a collection of love poems, but some of his poems are as exquisite as his short stories are horrific. Always an eccentric character, Poe was dismissed from West Point military academy for neglect of duty at the age of twenty-one. He subsequently pursued an erratic career as a journalist, fighting a lifelong battle against poverty, alcoholism and nervous instability. He appears never to have recovered from the death of his wife in 1847 and died in a Baltimore hospital having succumbed to (according to varying reports) either alcoholism, heart failure or epilepsy.*

ANNABEL LEE

It was many and many a year ago,
In a kingdom by the sea,

That a maiden there lived whom you may know
By the name of Annabel Lee;
And this maiden she lived with no other thought
Than to love and be loved by me.

She was a child and I was a child,
In this kingdom by the sea,
But we loved with a love that was more than love –
I and my Annabel Lee –
With a love that the wingèd seraphs of Heaven
Coveted her and me.

And this was the reason that, long ago,
In this kingdom by the sea,
A wind blew out of a cloud, by night
Chilling my Annabel Lee;
So that her highborn kinsmen came
And bore her away from me,
To shut her up in a sepulchre
In this kingdom by the sea.

The angels, not half so happy in Heaven,
Went envying her and me: –
Yes! – that was the reason (as all men know,
In this kingdom by the sea)
That the wind came out of the cloud, chilling
And killing my Annabel Lee.

But our love it was stronger by far than the love
Of those who were older than we –

Of many far wiser than we –
And neither the angels in Heaven above
Nor the demons down under the sea,
Can ever dissever my soul from the soul
Of the beautiful Annabel Lee: –

For the moon never beams, without bringing me dreams
Of the beautiful Annabel Lee;
And the stars never rise but I see the bright eyes
Of the beautiful Annabel Lee:
And so, all the night-tide, I lie down by the side
Of my darling, my darling, my life and my bride,
In the sepulchre there by the sea –
In her tomb by the side of the sea.

ROBERT BROWNING (1812-1889)

Browning outlived his wife by twenty-eight years, returning to England after her death. The realism of the best of his verse is a refreshing contrast to the by now hackneyed forms of Romanticism.

THE LOST MISTRESS

All's over, then: does truth sound bitter
As one at first believes?
Hark, 'tis the sparrows' good-night twitter
About your cottage eaves!

And the leaf-buds on the vine are woolly,
I noticed that, to-day;
One day more bursts them open fully
– You know the red turns gray.

To-morrow we meet the same then, dearest?
May I take your hand in mine?
Mere friends are we, – well, friends the merest
Keep much that I resign:

For each glance of the eye so bright and black,
Though I keep with heart's endeavour, –
Your voice, when you wish the snowdrops back,
Though it stay in my soul for ever! –

Yet I will but say what mere friends say,
Or only a thought stronger;
I will hold your hand but as long as all may,
Or so very little longer!

WALT WHITMAN (1819-1892)

The most remarkable figure in nineteenth-century American poetry, Whitman offended many people through his outspokenness on sexual matters. Although he is not generally considered a romantic poet, these two examples show that he was capable of expressing both intimacy and eroticism.

LOVE POETRY

As Adam Early in the Morning

As Adam early in the morning
Walking forth from the bower refresh'd with sleep,
Behold me where I pass, hear my voice, approach,
Touch me, touch the palm of your hand to my body as I pass,
Be not afraid of my body.

When I Heard at the Close of the Day

When I heard at the close of the day how my name had been receiv'd with
plaudits in the capitol, still it was not a happy night for me that follow'd,
And else when I carous'd, or when my plans were accomplish'd,
still I was not happy,
But the day when I rose at dawn from the bed of perfect health, refresh'd,
singing, inhaling the ripe breath of autumn,
When I saw the full moon in the west grow pale and disappear
in the morning light,
When I wander'd alone over the beach, and undressing bathed, laughing with
the cool waters, and saw the sun rise,
And when I thought how my dear friend my lover was on his way coming, O
then I was happy,
O then each breath tasted sweeter, and all that day my food nourish'd me more,
and the beautiful day pass'd well,
And the next came with equal joy, and with the next at evening came my friend,
And that night while all was still
I heard the waters roll slowly continually up the shores, I heard the hissing rustle
of the liquid and sands as directed to me whispering to congratulate me,

OPPOSITE. SELF-PORTRAIT, MARY ELLEN SARG

90

For the one I love most lay sleeping by me under the same cover in the cool night,

In the stillness in the autumn moonbeams his face was inclined toward me,

And his arm lay lightly around my breast – and that night I was happy.

HERMAN MELVILLE (1819-1891)

Melville spent his early twenties at sea, an experience which inspired much of his writing. He achieved critical acclaim but little popular success during his lifetime, and was forced to write what he considered 'potboilers' in order to support a large family. It was only after his death that Moby Dick *was hailed as an American classic.*

MONODY

To have known him, to have loved him
After loneness long;
And then to be estranged in life,
And neither in the wrong;
And now for death to set his seal
Ease me, a little ease, my song!

By wintry hills his hermit-mound
The sheeted snow-drifts drape,
And houseless there the snow-bird flits
Beneath the fir-trees' crape:
Glazed now with ice the cloistral vine
That hid the shyest grape.

❧❧❧

CHARLES BAUDELAIRE (1821-1867)

Born to wealth and social position, Baudelaire was a rebel from an early age and a social misfit throughout his life. He soon squandered his inheritance and spent the rest of his life in debt. A rebel, too, in his writing, he believed – in opposition to established French thought at the time – that an artist had total freedom of choice in both subject and treatment. He exemplified these views in his greatest work, Les Fleurs du Mal, *whose publication brought not only scandal but criminal prosecution because of the openly homosexual nature of some of the love poems. Although acquitted, he emerged from the ordeal a broken man and, ravaged by drink and opium, died only three years later.*
These extracts are all taken from Les Fleurs du Mal.

ALL IN ONE

The Demon called on me this morning,
In my high room. As is his way,
Thinking to catch me without warning,
He put this question: 'Tell me, pray,

Of all the beauties that compose,
The strange enchantment of her ways,
Amongst the wonders black or rose,
Which object most excites your praise,

And is the climax in her litany?'
My soul, you answered the Abhorred,
'Since she is fashioned, all, of dittany,
No part is most to be adored.

Since I am ravished, I ignore a
Degree of difference in delight.
She dazzles me like the aurora
And she consoles me like the night.

The harmony's so exquisite
That governs her, it is in vain
Analysis would try to split
The unity of such a strain.

O mystic fusion that, enwreathing
My senses, fuses each in each,
To hear the music of her breathing
And breathe the perfume of her speech.'

AUTUMN SONNET

Your eyes like crystal ask me, clear and mute,
'In me, strange lover, what do you admire?'
Be lovely: hush: my heart, whom all things tire
Except the candour of the primal brute,

Would hide from you the secret burning it
And its black legend written out in fire,
O soother of the sleep that I respire!
Passion I hate, and I am hurt by wit.

Let us love gently. In his lair laid low,
Ambushed in shades, Love strings his fatal bow.
I know his ancient arsenal complete,

PORTRAIT OF YEKATERINA AVDULINA, OREST KIPRENSKI

Crime, horror, lunacy – O my pale daisy!

Are we not suns in Autumn, silver-hazy,

O my so white, so snow-cold Marguerite?

EXOTIC FRAGRANCE

When, with closed eyes in the warm autumn night,

I breathe the fragrance of thy bosom bare,

My dream unfurls a clime of loveliest air,

Drenched in the fiery sun's unclouded light.

An indolent island dowered with heaven's delight,

Trees singular and fruits of savour rare,

Men having sinewy frames; robust and spare,

And women whose clear eyes are wondrous bright.

Led by thy fragrance to those shores I hail

A charmèd harbour thronged with mast and sail,

Still wearied with the quivering sea's unrest;

What time the scent of the green tamarinds

That thrills the air and fills my swelling breast

Blends with the mariners' song and the sea-winds.

ﻫﻬﻫ

Adelaide Anne Procter (1825-1864)

Adelaide Procter was raised in literary circles in London and knew Dickens and
Thackeray from an early age. She submitted her first poems to Dickens's magazine
Household Words under an assumed name, because she hoped that they would be
accepted on their merits rather than because she knew the editor. They were,
and she went on to achieve great popular success, although many of her
poems are too sentimental for modern tastes.

A Woman's Last Word

Well – the links are broken,
All is past;
This farewell, when spoken,
Is the last.
I have tried and striven
All in vain;
Such bonds must be riven,
Spite of pain,
And never, never, never
Knit again.

So I tell you plainly,
It must be:
I shall try, not vainly,
To be free;
Truer, happier chances
Wait me yet,

While you, through fresh fancies,

Can forget; –

And life has nobler uses

Than Regret.

All past words retracing,

One by one,

Does not help effacing

What is done.

Let it be. Oh, stronger

Links can break!

Had we dreamed still longer

We could wake, –

Yet let us part in kindness

For Love's sake.

Bitterness and sorrow

Will at last,

In some bright to-morrow,

Heal their past;

But future hearts will never

Be as true

As mine was – is ever,

Dear, for you…

Then must we part, when loving

As we do?

ॐ

ELIZABETH SIDDALL (?1829-1862)

Lizzie Siddall was an aspiring painter and poet when she met the great Pre-Raphaelite Dante Gabriel Rossetti, whose mistress, muse and eventually wife she became. She modelled for many of the 'Brotherhood's' paintings, notably Millais' drowned Ophelia. Having suffered from ill-health for some time, she died when in her early thirties, of an overdose of laudanum.

DEAD LOVE

Oh never weep for love that's dead
Since love is seldom true
But changes his fashion from blue to red,
From brightest red to blue,
And love was born to an early death
And is so seldom true.

Then harbour no smile on your bonny face
To win the deepest sigh.
The fairest words on truest lips
Pass on and surely die,
And you will stand alone, my dear,
When wintry winds draw nigh.

Sweet, never weep for what cannot be,
For this God has not given.
If the merest dream of love were true
Then, sweet, we should be in heaven,
And this is only earth, my dear,
Where true love is not given.

LOVE POETRY

Emily Dickinson (1830-1886)

Emily Dickinson led a quiet life at home in New England, and critics have often speculated as to whether she suffered a disappointment in love as a young woman. Many of her poems are decidedly religious in nature; some could be interpreted as referring to either spiritual or earthly love. These two are surely unambiguous.

I Taste a Liquor Never Brewed

I taste a liquor never brewed,
From tankards scooped in pearl;
Not all the vats upon the Rhine
Yield such an alcohol!

Inebriate of air am I,
And debauchee of dew,
Reeling, through endless summer days,
From inns of molten blue.

When landlords turn the drunken bee
Out of the foxglove's door,
When butterflies renounce their dram
I shall but drink the more!

'I Cannot Live with You'

I cannot live with You –
It would be Life –
And Life is over there –
Behind the Shelf

The Sexton keeps the Key to

Putting up

Our Life – His Porcelain –

Like a Cup –

AT THE SPRING, BIRKET FOSTER

Discarded of the Housewife –
Quaint – or Broke –
A newer Sevres pleases –
Old Ones crack –

I could not die – with You –
For One must wait –
To shut the Other's Gaze down –
You – could not –

And I – Could I stand by
And see You – freeze –
Without my Right of Frost –
Death's privilege?

Nor could I rise – with You –
Because Your Face
Would put out Jesus' –
That New Grace

Glow plain – and foreign
On my homesick Eye –
Except that You than He
Shone closer by –

They'd judge Us – How –
For You – served Heaven – You know,
Or sought to –
I could not –

Because You saturated Sight –
And I had no more Eyes
For sordid excellence
As Paradise

And were You lost, I would be –
Though My Name
Rang loudest
On the Heavenly fame –

And were You – saved –
And I – condemned to be
Where You were not –
That self – were Hell to Me –

So We must meet apart –
You there – I – here
With just the Door ajar
That Oceans are – and Prayer –
And that White Sustenance –
Despair –

CHRISTINA ROSSETTI (1830-94)

Christina Rossetti was the sister of Dante Gabriel Rossetti and spent her life on the fringes of the Pre-Raphaelite Brothernood of which he was a prominent member. She never married and the theme of unrequited or frustrated love which recurs frequently in her verse has led critics to speculate on an unhappy affair in her own life. Her work has a

strong sense of mysticism and, like Emily Dickinson, sometimes leaves her reader
wondering whether she is speaking of divine or earthly love.

SONG

When I am dead, my dearest,
Sing no sad songs for me;
Plant thou no roses at my head,
Nor shady cypress tree:
Be the green grass above me
With showers and dewdrops wet;
And if thou wilt, remember,
And if thou wilt, forget.

I shall not see the shadows,
I shall not feel the rain;
I shall not hear the nightingale
Sing on, as if in pain:
And dreaming through the twilight
That doth not rise nor set,
Haply I may remember,
And haply may forget.

ALGERNON CHARLES SWINBURNE (1837-1909)

A friend of Dante Gabriel Rossetti and William Morris, Swinburne travelled widely in
Europe during his youth, living a dissipated life that led to a breakdown, after which he

spent the rest of his years in near seclusion. Many of his poems are passionate and uninhibited, so much so that they offended some of their audience, but his first volume of Poems and Ballads *was immensely successful – the British public had not read anything so exciting for years.*

A Leave-Taking

Let us go hence, my songs; she will not hear.
Let us go hence together without fear;
Keep silence now, for singing-time is over,
And over all old things and all things dear.
She loves not you nor me as we all love her.
Yea, though we sang as angels in her ear,
She would not hear.

Let us rise up and part; she will not know.
Let us go seaward as the great winds go,
Full of blown sand and foam; what help is here?
There is no help, for all these things are so,
And all the world is bitter as a tear.
And how these things are, though ye strove to show,
She would not know.

Let us go home and hence; she will not weep.
We gave love many dreams and days to keep,
Flowers without scent, and fruits that would not grow,
Saying, 'If thou wilt, thrust in thy sickle and reap.'
All is reaped now; no grass is left to mow;
And we that sowed, though all we fell on sleep,
She would not weep.

Let us go hence and rest; she will not love.

She shall not hear us if we sing hereof,

Nor see love's ways, how sore they are and steep.

Come hence, let be, lie still; it is enough.

Love is a barren sea, bitter and deep;

And though she saw all heaven in flower above,

She would not love.

Let us give up, go down; she will not care.

Though all the stars made gold of all the air,

And the sea moving saw before it move

One moon-flower making all the foam-flowers fair;

Though all those waves went over us, and drove

Deep down the stifling lips and drowning hair,

She would not care.

Let us go hence, go hence; she will not see.

Sing all once more together; surely she,

She too, remembering days and words that were,

Will turn a little toward us, sighing; but we,

We are hence, we are gone, as though we had not been there.

Nay, and though all men seeing had pity on me,

She would not see.

THOMAS HARDY (1840-1928)

Born in Dorchester, Dorset – Casterbridge in his novel The Mayor of Casterbridge *–
Hardy spent most of his life in his beloved Wessex. He became immensely successful in*

his lifetime, despite the critics' dislike of the 'pessimism' and 'immorality' of Tess of the d'Urbervilles *and* Jude the Obscure. *Jude was, in fact, his last novel – after the furore that greeted its publication*

THE ARTIST'S SISTER, VICTOR BORISOV-MUSATOV (DETAIL)

in 1895, Hardy turned largely to poetry. His first marriage, to
Emma Gifford, is known to have been turbulent, and some of his best verses
were written after Emma's death in 1912.

THE VOICE

Woman much missed, how you call to me, call to me,
Saying that now you are not as you were
When you had changed from the one who was all to me,
But as at first, when our day was fair.

Can it be you that I hear? Let me view you, then,
Standing as when I drew near to the town
Where you would wait for me: yes, as I knew you then,
Even to the original air-blue gown!

Or is it only the breeze, in its listlessness
Travelling across the wet mead to me here,
You being ever dissolved to wan wistlessness,
Heard no more again far or near?

Thus I; faltering forward,
Leaves around me falling,
Wind oozing thin through the thorn from norward,
And the woman calling.

❧❧

A Thunderstorm in Town

She wore a new 'terra-cotta' dress,
And we stayed, because of the pelting storm,
Within the hansom's dry recess,
Though the horse had stopped; yea, motionless
We sat on, snug and warm.

Then the downpour ceased, to my sharp sad pain
And the glass that had screened our forms before
Flew up, and out she sprang to her door:
I should have kissed her if the rain
Had lasted a minute more.

Paul Verlaine (1844-1896)

Verlaine lived a Bohemian and frequently scandalous life – one contemporary
critic remarked that 'perhaps no living poet has had a more intimate
acquaintance with the seamy side of life'. Escaping from Paris to Brussels
because he found married life intolerable, he became involved with
the young poet, Arthur Rimbaud. The scandal that surrounded Rimbaud's
attempts to end this relationship led to Verlaine's being sentenced to two
years' hard labour for 'immorality'. He ended his life in poverty, supporting
himself as best he could with lecture tours.
Despite – or perhaps because of – the upheavals of his personal life,
his poetry ranks among the most beautiful and lyrical
that France has produced.

WEARINESS

(For battles of love a field of down)

Soft, soft, I pray, sweet heart that pants and presses!
Oh calm awhile those feverish ecstasies!
Even at the height of transport she is wise
Whose warmth a sister's tranquil love confesses.

Be languishing! And lull me with your sighs,
As with your slumberous looks and slow caresses;
Not the fierce clasp nor the spasm that possesses
Is worth one lingering kiss, even one that lies!

But, in your golden heart, you say, dear child,
Love blows her oliphant with longings wild!…
There let the gipsy trumpet in her fashion!

Lay on my brow your brow, your hand in mine,
Breathe vows, to break them with the morrow's shine,
And let us weep till dawn, O soul of passion!

EMILY HICKEY (1845-1924)

*Emily Hickey was born in County Wexford, Ireland, and was one of
the founders of the Browning Society, in addition to publishing
a number of volumes of her own verse.*

A WEAK-MINDED WOMAN'S COMPARISONS

Well, with whom shall I compare you, seeing, O my lief and dear,
How to one (weak-minded!) woman you are just without a peer?
Nay, there is no need to tell me; for I know you deprecate,
Proving thus at least your greatness, anyone should call you great.
What, sir? 'tis the sheerest nonsense, well I know?
I'll not contradict your worship! Be it so!

Only I have caught you now, and do not mean to let you stir
Till I've told you things that, maybe, you will laugh at, frown at, sir.
Ay, comparisons are odious! so, in very sooth, they are!
You shall be compared with – whom then? no one in particular!
Just another – quite impersonal, you know – For convenience, any other; be it so!

I would rather have your tempest than another's radiant calm;
I would rather you should wound me than another bring me balm;
I would rather take your blame than praise from any other one;
Rather go in the dark with you than with another in the sun.
It's the very height of foolishness, I know;
But (consider I'm weak-minded!) it is so.

I would rather have your weakness than their strength men call the strong:
Let them do their rightest right, and I would rather have your wrong:
Wrong or right, my soul's beloved, yea, whatever you may do,
All my faith is clasped around you, and my whole soul loveth you.
That's the height of immorality, I know;
All the same, and notwithstanding, it is so!

But away with over-earnest; let us back to dainty jest!

Is the jest, or is the earnest, tell me, dear my lord, the best?

Is it very gracious fooling, or the way of love to me,

Who am no enfranchised woman of the twentieth century,

But a poor weak-minded creature, and, you know,

'Tis no more, as some one says, no more but so.

GUY DE MAUPASSANT (1850-1893)

One of the best short story writers of all time, Maupassant's prose style is realistic and witty, but his single collection of poems has been described as 'deliberately cold and calm'. In the last years of his life he was tortured by insanity and died in an asylum.

DESIRES

The dream of one is to have wings and follow

The soaring heights of space. with clamorous cries;

With lissome fingers seize the supple swallow

And lose himself in sombre gulfs of skies.

Another would have strength with circling shoulder

To crush the wrestler in his close embrace;

And, not with yielding loins or blood grown colder,

Stop, with one stroke, wild steeds in frantic chase.

What I love best is loveliness corporeal:

I would be beautiful as gods of old;

So from my radiant limbs love immemorial
In hearts of men a living flame should hold.

I would have women love me in wild fashion –
Choose one to-day and with to-morrow change;
Pleased, when I pass, to pluck the flower of passion,
As fruits are plucked when forth the fingers range.

Each leaves upon the lips a different flavour;
These diverse savours bid their sweetness grow.
My fond caress would fly with wandering favour
From dusky locks to locks of golden glow.

But most of all I love the unlooked-for meeting,
Those ardours in the blood loosed by a glance,
The conquests of an hour, as swiftly fleeting,
Kisses exchanged at the sole will of chance.

At daybreak I would dote on the dark charmer,
Whose clasping arms cling close in amorous swoon
And, lulled at eve by the blonde siren's murmur,
Gaze on her pale brow silvered by the moon.

Then my calm heart, that holds no haunting spectre,
Would lightly towards a fresh chimera haste:
Enough in these delights to sip the nectar,
For in the dregs there lurks a bitter taste.

༄༅

LOVE POETRY

OSCAR WILDE (1854-1900)

Oscar Wilde's notorious affair with Lord Alfred Douglas brought him personal sorrow and public disgrace. His poems often reflect the bitterness he felt on the subject of love.

HÉLAS

To drift with every passion till my soul
Is a stringèd lute on which all winds can play,
Is it for this that I have given away
Mine ancient wisdom, and austere control?
Methinks my life is a twice-written scroll
Scrawled over on some boyish holiday!
With idle songs for pipe and virelay,
Which do but mar the secret of the whole.
Surely there was a time I might have trod
The sunlit heights, and from life's dissonance
Struck one clear chord to reach the ears of God:
Is that time dead? Lo! with a little rod
I did but touch the honey of romance –
And must I lose a soul's inheritance?

CONSTANCE NADEN (1858-1889)

Constance Naden was born and educated in Birmingham in the English Midlands. As a student, she excelled at logic and science. Becoming a supporter of women's suffrage thirty years before this became a much-publicised campaign, she also wrote on evolution

REAPERS, ALEXEI VENETSIANOV

and other scientific and philosophical subjects. She published only two books of verse,
having come to consider the writing of poetry as 'a mere amusement'.

LOVE VERSUS LEARNING

Alas, for the blight of my fancies!
Alas, for the fall of my pride!
I planned, in my girlish romances,
To be a philosopher's bride.

I pictured him leamed and witty,
The sage and the lover combined,
Not scoming to say I was pretty,
Nor only adoring my mind.

No elderly, spectacled Mentor,
But one who would worship and woo;
Perhaps I might take an inventor,
Or even a poet would do.

And tender and gay and well-favoured,
My fate overtook me at last:
I saw, and I heard, and I wavered,
I smiled, and my freedom was past.

He promised to love me for ever,
He pleaded, and what could I say?
I thought he must surely be clever,
For he is an Oxford M.A.

But now, I begin to discover
My visions are fatally marred;
Perfection itself as a lover,
He's neither a sage nor a bard.

He's mastered the usual knowledge,
And says it's a terrible bore;
He formed his opinions at college,
Then why should he think any more?

My logic he sets at defiance,
Declares that my Latin's no use,
And when I begin to talk Science
He calls me a dear little goose.

He says that my lips are too rosy
To speak in a language that's dead,
And all that is dismal and prosy
Should fly from so sunny a head.

He scoffs at each grave occupation,
Turns everything off with a pun;
And says that his sole calculation
Is how to make two into one.

He says Mathematics may vary,
Geometry cease to be true,
But scorning the slightest vagary
He still will continue to woo.

He says that the sun may stop action,
But he will not swerve from his course;
For love is his law of attraction,
A smile his centripetal force.

His levity's truly terrific,
And often I think we must part,
But compliments so scientific
Recapture my fluttering heart.

Yet sometimes 'tis very confusing
This conflict of love and of lore
But hark! I must cease from my musing
For that is his knock at the door!

E. NESBIT (1858-1924)

Edith Nesbit spent much of her adult life in an unconventional ménage à trois in South London. Her books for children, of which the best known is The Railway Children, *and her poetry are distinguished by a wry sense of humour and lack of sentimentality that sets her apart from many of her Victorian contemporaries.*

INDISCRETION

Red tulip-buds last night caressed
The sacred ivory of her breast.
She met me, eager to divine
What gold-heart bud of hope was mine.

Nor eyes nor lips were strong to part

The close-curled petals round my heart;

The joy I knew no monarch knows,

Yet not a petal would unclose.

But, ah! – the tulip-buds, unwise,

Warmed with the sunshine of her eyes,

And by her soft breath glorified,

Went mad with love and opened wide.

She saw their hearts, all golden-gay,

Laughed, frowned, and flung the flowers away.

Poor flowers, in Heaven as you were,

Why did you show your hearts to her?

RABINDRANATH TAGORE (1861-1941)

*A poet, playwright, painter, educator and musician, Rabindranath Tagore also became a
leading figure in the Indian nationalist movement, working closely with Gandhi.
Much admired by the poets W.B Yeats, Ezra Pound, Alice Meynell and by the painter
William Rothenstein who were instrumental in having the first of his work
in English translation –* Gitanjeli *– published by Macmillan in 1912.
In 1913 Tagore was awarded the Nobel Prize for Literature.*

UNENDING LOVE

I seem to have loved you in numberless forms, numberless times,

In life after life, in age after age forever.

My spell-bound heart has made and re-made the necklace of songs
That you take as a gift, wear round your neck in your many forms
In life after life, in age after age forever.

Whenever I hear old chronicles of love, its age-old pain,
Its ancient tale of being apart or together,
As I stare on and on into the past, in the end you emerge
Clad in the light of a pole-star piercing the darkness of time:
You become an image of what is remembered forever.

You and I have floated here on the stream that brings from the fount
At the heart of time love of one for another.
We have played alongside millions of lovers, shared in the same
Shy sweetness of meeting, the same distressful tears of farewell
Old love, but in shapes that renew and renew forever.

Today it is heaped at your feet, it has found its end in you,
The love of all man's days both past and forever:
Universal joy, universal sorrow, universal life,
The memories of all loves merging with this one love of ours
And the songs of every poet past and forever.

W. B. YEATS (1865-1939)

William Butler Yeats is one of the most important figures in the history of Irish literature, and has had an immense influence on every following generation of poets.

OPPOSITE. FLOWERS, JAN BRUEGHELS

120

Much of his work was inspired by his passion for his fellow Republican Maud Gonne,
but this poem is based on a sonnet by Ronsard (see page 34).

WHEN YOU ARE OLD

When you are old and gray and full of sleep
And nodding by the fire, take down this book,
And slowly read, and dream of the soft look
Your eyes had once, and of their shadows deep;

How many loved your moments of glad grace,
And loved your beauty with love false or true;
But one man loved the pilgrim soul in you,
And loved the sorrows of your changing face.

And bending down beside the glowing bars,
Murmur, a little sadly, how love fled
And paced upon the mountains overhead,
And hid his face amid a crowd of stars.

ERNEST DOWSON (1867-1900)

Dowson belonged to the so-called Decadent School of the late nineteenth century
and was a friend of Oscar Wilde and the artist Aubrey Beardsley.
Many of his poems exhibit a certain world-weariness,
but he was also capable of genuine emotion.

LOVE POETRY

Nₒₙ ...

Nᴏɴ sᴜᴍ ǫᴜᴀʟɪs ᴇʀᴀᴍ ʙᴏɴᴀᴇ sᴜʙ ʀᴇɢɴᴏ Cʏɴᴀʀᴀᴇ
(I am not what I was under the reign of the good Cynara)

Last night, ah, yesternight, betwixt her lips and mine
There fell thy shadow, Cynara! thy breath was shed
Upon my soul between the kisses and the wine;
And I was desolate and sick of an old passion,
Yea, I was desolate and bowed my head:
I have been faithful to thee, Cynara! in my fashion.

All night upon mine heart I felt her warm heart beat,
Night-long within mine arms in love and sleep she lay;
Surely the kisses of her bought red mouth were sweet;
But I was desolate and sick of an old passion,
When I awoke and found the dawn was gray:
I have been faithful to thee, Cynara! in my fashion.

I have forgot much, Cynara! gone with the wind,
Flung roses, roses riotously with the throng,
Dancing, to put thy pale, lost lilies out of mind;
But I was desolate and sick of an old passion,
Yea, all the time, because the dance was long:
I have been faithful to thee, Cynara! in my fashion.

I cried for madder music and for stronger wine,
But when the feast is finished and the lamps expire,
Then falls thy shadow, Cynara! the night is thine;
And I am desolate and sick of an old passion,
Yea, hungry for the lips of my desire:
I have been faithful to thee, Cynara! in my fashion.

BEYOND

Love's aftermath! I think the time is now
That we must gather in, alone, apart
The saddest crop of all the crops that grow,
Love's aftermath.
Ah sweet, – sweet yesterday, the tears that start
Can not put back the dial, this is, I trow,
Our harvesting! Thy kisses chill my heart,
Our lips are cold; averted eyes avow
The twilight of poor love; we can but part
Dumbly and sadly, reaping as we sow,
Love's aftermath.

JOHN MILLINGTON SYNGE (1871-1909)

Better known as a playwright, Synge was born near Dublin and became a director of the Abbey Theatre, where a number of his controversial plays, notably The Playboy of the Western World, *were performed. He died young, having suffered for some years from Hodgkins' disease.*

WITH ONE LONG KISS

With one long kiss
Were you nearby
You'd break the dismal cloud that is
On all my sky.

LOVE POETRY

With one long kiss

If you were near

You'd sweeten days I take amiss

When lonely here.

ELDERLY COUPLE, ANONYMOUS RUSSIAN PAINTER

With one long kiss
You'd make for me
A golden paradise of this
Day's beggary.

AMY LOWELL (1874-1925)

Like Emily Dickinson, Amy Lowell came from a prosperous New England background. Unlike her great predecessor, however, she was not content to sit quietly at home and write. Instead she became prominent in literary circles, gave lectures and readings across the United States and campaigned tirelessly to make poetry more widely read. **Patterns** *is her best-known poem.*

PATTERNS

I walk down the garden paths,
And all the daffodils
Are blowing, and the bright blue squills.
I walk down the patterned garden-paths
In my stiff, brocaded gown
With my powdered hair and jewelled fan,
I too am a rare
Pattern. As I wander down
The garden paths.

My dress is richly figured,
And the train

Makes a pink and silver stain

On the gravel, and the thrift

Of the borders.

Just a plate of current fashion,

Tripping by in high-heeled, ribboned shoes.

Not a softness anywhere about me,

Only whalebone and brocade.

And I sink on a seat in the shade

Of a lime tree. For my passion

Wars against the stiff brocade.

The daffodils and squills

Flutter in the breeze

As they please.

And I weep;

For the lime tree is in blossom

And one small flower has dropped upon my bosom.

And the splashing of waterdrops

In the marble fountain

Comes down the garden-paths.

The dripping never stops.

Underneath my stiffened gown

Is the softness of a woman bathing in a marble basin

A basin in the midst of hedges grown

So thick, she cannot see her lover hiding,

But she guesses he is near,

And the sliding of the water

Seems the stroking of a dear

Hand upon her.

What is Summer in a fine brocaded gown!

I should like to see it lying in a heap upon the ground.
All the pink and silver crumpled up on the ground.

I would be the pink and silver as I ran along the path
And he would stumble after,
Bewildered by my laughter.
I should see the sun flashing from his sword-hilt and the buckles on his shoes.
I would choose
To lead him in a maze along the patterned paths,
A bright and laughing maze for my heavy-booted lover.
Till he caught me in the shade,
And the buttons of his waistcoat bruised my body as he clasped me,
Aching, melting, unafraid.
With the shadows of the leaves and the sundrops,
And the plopping of the waterdrops,
All about us in the open afternoon –
I am very like to swoon
With the weight of this brocade,
For the sun sifts through the shade.

Underneath the fallen blossom
In my bosom,
Is a letter I have hid.
It was brought to me this morning by a rider from the Duke.
'Madam, we regret to inform you that Lord Hartwell
Died in action Thursday se'nnight.'
As I read it in the white, morning sunlight,
The letters squirmed like snakes.
'Any answer, Madam' said my footman.

OPPOSITE. THE RIDING HABIT, MIKHAIL NESTEROV

'No' I told him.

'See that the messenger takes some refreshment.

No, no answer.'

And I walked into the garden,

Up and down the patterned paths,

In my stiff, correct brocade.

The blue and yellow flowers stood up proudly in the sun,

Each one.

I stood upright too,

Held rigid to the pattern

By the stiffness of my gown.

Up and down I walked,

Up and down.

In a month he would have been my husband.

In a month, here, underneath this lime,

We would have broke the pattern;

He for me and I for him,

He as Colonel, I as Lady,

On this shady seat.

He had a whim

That sunlight carried blessing.

And I answered, 'It shall be as you have said.'

Now he is dead.

In Summer and in Winter I shall walk

Up and down

The patterned garden-paths

In my stiff, brocaded gown.

The squills and daffodils

Will give place to pillared roses, and to asters, and to snow.

I shall go

Up and down,

In my gown.

Gorgeously arrayed,

Boned and stayed.

And the softness of my body will be guarded from embrace

By each button, hook and lace.

For the man who should loose me is dead.

Fighting with the Duke in Flanders,

In a pattern called a war.

Christ! What are patterns for?

SAROJINI NAIDU (1878-1949)

Sarojini Naidu was born and brought up in Hyderabad, in a household where she was taught to be an Indian and a citizen of the world, not just a Hindu. She published her first volume of verse when she was sixteen and three further collections in the course of the next twenty years. She was deeply involved in the independence struggle of India, taking part in Gandhi's famous Salt March in 1930. She was appointed Governor of the state of Uttar Pradesh on Indian Independence in 1947.

THE TEMPLE, A PILGRIMAGE OF LOVE (extracts)

I

Were beauty mine, Beloved, I would bring it

Like a rare blossom to Love's glowing shrine;

Were a dear youth mine, Beloved, I would fling it
Like a rich pearl into Love's lustrous wine.

Were greatness mine, Beloved, I would offer
Such radiant gifts of glory and of fame,
Like camphor and like curds to pour and proffer
Before Love's right and sacrificial flame.

But I have naught save my heart's deathless passion
That craves no recompense divinely sweet,
Content to wait in proud and lowly fashion,
And kiss the shadow of Love's passing feet.

II
Bring no fragrant sandal paste,
Let me gather Love instead.
The entranced and flowering dust
You have honoured with your tread
For mine eyelids and mine head.

Bring no scented lotus wreath,
Moon-awakened, dew-caressed
Love, thro' memory's age-long dream,
Sweeter shall my wild heart rest
With your footprints on my breast.

Bring no pearls from ravished seas,
Gems from rifled hemispheres;
Grant me, Love, in priceless boon
All the sorrow of your years,
All the secret of your tears.

V

If you call me I will come
Swifter, O my Love,
Than a trembling forest deer
Or a panting dove,
Swifter than a snake that flies
To the charmer's thrall. . .
If you call me I will come
Fearless what befall.

If you call me I will come
Swifter than desire,
Swifter than the lightning's feet
Shod with plumes of fire.
Life's dark tides may roll between,
Or Death's deep chasms divide –
If you call me I will come
Fearless what betide.

D. H. LAWRENCE (1885-1930)

David Herbert Lawrence is best known for his novels, but the passion of Lady
Chatterley's Lover *and* Sons and Lovers *re-emerges in his magnificent poetry.*

THE BRIDE

My love looks like a girl to-night,
But she is old.

The plaits that lie along her pillow
Are not gold,
But threaded with filigree silver,
And uncanny cold.

She looks like a young maiden, since her brow
Is smooth and fair;
Her cheeks are very smooth, her eyes are closed,
She sleeps a rare,
Still, winsome sleep, so still, and so composed.

Nay, but she sleeps like a bride, and dreams her dreams
Of perfect things.
She lies at last, the darling, in the shape of her dream;
And her dead mouth sings
By its shape, like thrushes in clear evenings.

BOTH SIDES OF THE MEDAL

And because you love me,
think you you do not hate me?
Ha, since you love me
to ecstasy
it follows you hate me to ecstasy.

Because when you hear me
go down the road outside the house
you must come to the window to watch me go,
do you think it is pure worship?

Because, when I sit in the room,

here, in my own house,

and you want to enlarge yourself with this friend of mine,

such a friend as he is,

yet you cannot get beyond your awareness of me,

SOLITUDE, HARRIET BACKER

you are held back by my being in the same world with you,

do you think it is bliss alone?

sheer harmony?

No doubt if I were dead, you must

reach into death after me,

but would not your hate reach even more madly than your love?

your impassioned, unfinished hate?

Since you have a passion for me,

as I for you,

does not that passion stand in your way like a Balaam's ass?

and am I not Balaam's ass

golden-mouthed occasionally?

But mostly, do you not detest my bray?

Since you are confined in the orbit of me

do you not loathe the confinement?

Is not even the beauty and peace of an orbit

an intolerable prison to you,

as it is to everybody?

But we will learn to submit

each of us to the balanced, eternal orbit

wherein we circle on our fate

in strange conjunction.

What is chaos, my love?

It is not freedom.

A disarray of falling stars coming to nought.

LOVE POETRY

E E CUMMINGS (1894-1962)

Edward Estlin Cummings established his literary reputation with an account of the three months he spent in a French detention camp in 1917. His poetry attracted attention for its unorthodox style (such as the refusal to use capital letters) and its uninhibited subject matter.

my sweet old etcetera
aunt lucy during the recent

war could and what
is more did tell you just
what everybody was fighting

for,
my sister

isabel created hundreds
(and
hundreds)of socks not to
mention shirts fleaproof earwarmers

etcetera wristers etcetera,my

mother hoped that

i would die etcetera
bravely of course my father used
to become hoarse talking about how it was

a privilege and if only he
could meanwhile my

self etcetetera lay quietly
in the deep mud et

cetera
(dreaming,
et
cetera,of
Your smile
eyes knees and of your Etcetera)

JUANA DE IBARBOUROU (1895-1979)

*Juana de Ibarbourou was born in Uruguay and her poetry has all the exhuberant
spontaneity of a woman in love. Her beloved husband died in 1942 and the poetry of her
later years expresses her sorrow, combined with images of old age and death and
contrasting them with the joys of youth and passionate love. She is still widely acclaimed
in Latin America and in 1929 was lauded as 'Juana de América' at a gala organised in
the city of Montevideo, where she lived since 1929 until her death.*

DAWN

I have spent a restless and sleepless night.
Day is dawning and I slip out of bed, bored.
Today I alone walk along this long street
of sealed doors and sleeping houses.

A dawn like smoke.

It seems the sun, ill-humored,

has lit a fire with green wood

to cook its breakfast.

The wind is moist like it just came from

a bath. In the pale sky,

the colorless stars

little by little are vanishing.

A milkman in a red beret goes by.

From atop an old wall,

I am tempted by a bent, plush branch

heavy with ripe medlars.

I walk, walk, walk, walk.

When I return and bend over him

With a kiss, to wake him,

He will think, with hungry joy,

That I too have just come from the bath.

FEDERICO GARCÍA LORCA (1898-1936)

One of the great figures of twentieth-century Spanish literature, Lorca was acclaimed for
his passionate plays and poetry, especially the Romancero gitano, *which celebrated*
the Spanish gypsy tradition. He was killed – probably murdered by
Nationalists – at the start of the Spanish Civil War.

SERENADE

(Homage to Lope de Vega)

Along the banks of the river
the night is getting wet
and on the breasts of Lolita
the branches are dying of love.

The branches are dying of love.

The night is singing naked
over the bridges of March.
Lolita is washing her body
with brackish water and nards.

The branches are dying of love.

The night of anise and silver
glares on the rooftops.
Silver of streams and mirrors.
Anise of your white thighs.

The branches are dying of love.

PABLO NERUDA (1904-1973)

The great Chilean poet was also a widely travelled diplomat and, for the last thirty years of his life, a Communist activist. He was awarded the Nobel Prize for Literature in 1971.

PORTRAIT OF A WOMAN, NATHAN ALTMAN

Much of his later work is political in nature, but he also wrote touching and often openly erotic love poems. This one is taken from his collection: Canto General.

YOUTH

A perfume like an acid sword
of plums on a road,
the kisses of sugar on your teeth,
the vital drops sliding on your fingers,
the sweet erotic pulp,
the gardens, the haylofts, the inciting
secret places in the huge houses,
the mattresses asleep in the past, the bitter green valley
seen from above, from the hidden glass:
all adolescence getting wet and burning
like an oil lamp dropped in the rain.

JOHN BETJEMAN (1906-1984)

Betjeman was one of the best loved English poets of the twentieth century, partly because he was also a television personality, presenting with great enthusiasm programmes on British architecture; and partly because his poetry was so easy to read and enjoy.
He became Poet Laureate in 1972.

A SUBALTERN'S LOVE-SONG

Miss J. Hunter Dunn, Miss J. Hunter Dunn,
Furnish'd and burnish'd by Aldershot sun,
What strenuous singles we played after tea,
We in the tournament – you against me!

Love-thirty, love-forty, oh! weakness of joy,
The speed of a swallow, the grace of a boy,
With carefullest carelessness, gaily you won,
I am weak from your loveliness, Joan Hunter Dunn.

Miss Joan Hunter Dunn, Miss Joan Hunter Dunn
How mad I am, sad I am, glad that you won.
The warm-handled racket is back in its press,
But my shock-headed victor, she loves me no less.

Her father's euonymus shines as we walk,
And swing past the summer-house, buried in talk
And cool the verandah that welcomes us in
To the six-o'clock news and a limejuice and gin.

The scent of the conifers, sound of the bath,
The view from my bedroom of moss-dappled path,
As I struggle with double-end evening tie,
For we dance at the Golf Club, my victor and I.

On the floor of her bedroom lie blazer and shorts
And the cream-coloured walls are be-trophied with sports,
And westering, questioning settles the sun

On your low-leaded window, Miss Joan Hunter Dunn.

The Hillman is waiting, the light's in the hall,
The pictures of Egypt are bright on the wall,
My sweet, I am standing beside the oak stair
And there on the landing's the light on your hair.

By roads 'not adopted', by woodlanded ways,
She drove to the club in the late summer haze,
Into nine-o'clock Camberley, heavy with bells
And mushroomy, pine-woody, evergreen smells.

Miss Joan Hunter Dunn, Miss Joan Hunter Dunn,
I can hear from the car-park the dance has begun.
Oh! full Surrey twilight! importunate band!
Oh! strongly adorable tennis-girl's hand!

Around us are Rovers and Austins afar,
Above us, the intimate roof of the car
And here on my right is the girl of my choice,
With the tilt of her nose and the chime of her voice,

And the scent of her wrap, and the words never said,
And the ominous, ominous dancing ahead.
We sat in the car park till twenty to one
And now I'm engaged to Miss Joan Hunter Dunn.

LOVE POETRY

Louis MacNeice (1907-1963)

Louis MacNeice was born in Belfast and became a friend of W. H. Auden and Stephen Spender. In his lifetime he was known as an accomplished writer of radio plays, but his posthumous reputation is based on his poetic work.

Meeting Point

Time was away and somewhere else,
There were two glasses and two chairs
And two people with the one pulse
(Somebody stopped the moving stairs):
Time was away and somewhere else.

And they were neither up nor down;
The stream's music did not stop
Flowing through heather, limpid brown,
Although they sat in a coffee shop
And they were neither up nor down.

The bell was silent in the air
Holding its inverted poise
Between a clang and clang a flower,
A brazen calyx of no noise:
The bell was silent in the air.

The camels crossed the miles of sand
That stretched around the cups and plates;
The desert was their own, they planned
To portion out the stars and dates:
The camels crossed the miles of sand.

Time was away and somewhere else.

The waiter did not come, the clock

Forgot them and the radio waltz

Came out like water from a rock:

Time was away and somewhere else.

Her fingers flicked away the ash

That bloomed again in tropic trees:

Not caring if the markets crash

When they had forests such as these,

Her fingers flicked away the ash.

God or whatever means the Good

Be praised that time can stop like this,

That what the heart has understood

Can verify in the body's peace

God or whatever means the Good.

Time was away and she was here

And life no longer than it was,

The bell was silent in the air

And all the room one glow because

Time was away and she was here.

EDWIN MORGAN (1920-)

Edwin Morgan was born in Glasgow and educated at Glasgow University. He later returned there as a lecturer in English, retiring as titular professor in 1980. The title of his 1972 collection **From Glasgow to Saturn** *gives some idea of the range of his work. He is the official Poet Laureate of Glasgow and was awarded the Queen's Gold Award for Poetry in 2000, the year of his eightieth birthday.*

STRAWBERRIES

There were never strawberries
like the ones we had
that sultry afternoon
sitting on the step
of the open french window
facing each other
your knees held in mine
the blue plates in our laps
the strawberries glistening
in the hot sunlight
we dipped them in sugar
looking at each other
not hurrying the feast
for one to come
the empty plates
laid on the stone together
with the two forks crossed
and I bent towards you
sweet in that air
in my arms
abandoned like a child
from your eager mouth
the taste of strawberries

in my memory

lean back again

let me love you

let the sun beat

on our forgefulness

one hour of all

the heat intense

and summer lightning

on the Kilpatrick hills

let the storm wash the plates.

ANNE SEXTON (1928-1974)

Born in Masschusetts, Anne Sexton suffered twenty years of mental illness after the birth
of her first child and ended, like her friend Sylvia Plath, by taking her own life .

FOR MY LOVER, RETURNING TO HIS WIFE

She is all there.

She was melted carefully down for you

and cast up from your childhood,

cast up from your one hundred favorite aggies.

She has always been there, my darling.

She is, in fact, exquisite.

STILL LIFE WITH FRUIT, OPEN BOOK, NATALIA GONCHAROVA

Fireworks in the dull middle of February
and as real as a cast-iron pot.

Let's face it, I have been momentary.
A luxury. A bright red sloop in the harbor.
My hair rising like smoke from the car window.
Littleneck clams out of season.

She is more than that. She is your have to have,
has grown you your practical your tropical growth.
This is not an experiment. She is all harmony.
She sees to oars and oarlocks for the dinghy,

has placed wild flowers at the window at breakfast,
sat by the potter's wheel at midday,
set forth three children under the moon,
three cherubs drawn by Michelangelo,

done this with her legs spread out
in the terrible months in the chapel.
If you glance up, the children are there
like delicate balloons resting on the ceiling.

She has also carried each one down the hall
after supper, their heads privately bent,
two legs protesting, person to person,
her face flushed with a song and their little sleep.

I give you back your heart.
I give you permission –
for the fuse inside her,

throbbing angrily in the dirt, for the bitch in her

and the burying of her wound –

for the burying of her small red wound alive –

for the pale flickering flare under her ribs,

for the drunken sailor who waits in her left pulse,

for the mother's knee, for the stockings,

for the garter belt, for the call –

the curious call

when you will burrow in arms and breasts

and tug at the orange ribbon in her hair

and answer the call, the curious call.

She is so naked and singular.

She is the sum of yourself and your dream.

Climb her like a monument, step after step.

She is solid.

As for me, I am a watercolor.

I wash off.

JENNY JOSEPH (1932-)

Jenny Joseph is best known for 'Warning' ('When I am an old woman I shall wear purple'), which the British public voted its favourite modern poem in 1996. This poem combines the same matter-of-fact tone with a passionate theme.

LOVE POETRY

THE SUN HAS BURST THE SKY

The sun has burst the sky
Because I love you
And the river its banks.

The sea laps the great rocks
Because I love you
And takes no heed of the moon dragging it away
And saying coldly 'Constancy is not for you.'

The blackbird fills the air
Because I love you
With spring and lawns and shadows falling on lawns.

The people walk in the street and laugh
I love you
And far down the river ships sound their hooters
Crazy with joy because I love you.

JAMES FENTON (1949-)

In addition to being a distinguished poet and a Fellow of the Royal Society of Literature, James Fenton has been a foreign correspondent whose experiences in South-East Asia are published under the title All the Wrong Places. *His varied career also includes theatre criticism and writing some of the libretto for* Les Misérables.

NOTHING

I take a jewel from a junk-shop tray
And wish I had a love to buy it for.
Nothing I choose will make you turn my way.
Nothing I give will make you love me more.
I know that I've embarrassed you too long
And I'm ashamed to linger at your door.
Whatever I embark on will be wrong.
Nothing I do will make you love me more.

I cannot work. I cannot read or write.
How can I frame a letter to implore.
Eloquence is a lie. The truth is trite.
Nothing I say will make you love me more.

So I replace the jewel in the tray
And laughingly pretend I'm far too poor.
Nothing I give, nothing I do or say,
Nothing I am will make you love me more.

INDEX OF FIRST LINES

Acknowledgements

'A Subalterne's Love Song' from *Collected Poems* by **John Betjeman**, by permission of John Murray (Publishers) Ltd. 'my sweet old etcetera' from *Complete Poems 1904-1962* by **E. E. Cummings** is reprinted by permission of W.W. Norton & Company Ltd. 'Nothing' by **James Fenton**. Reprinted by permission of PFD on behalf of James Fenton, ©: as printed in the original volume. 'Serenade' from *Obras completas* by **Federico García Lorca**, by permission of the translator, Michael Sanchez Brown © 2001, and of Aguilar, S.A. de Ediciones, Madrid © 1965. 'Dawn' from *Obras completas* by **Juana de Ibarbourou**, by permission of the translator, Michael Sanchez Brown © 2001, and of Aguilar, S.A. de Ediciones, Madrid © 1953.